"Black humor that effectively mixes comedy and tragedy. . . . This is satire at its best."—*The Jewish Journal*

"George Tabb's strength springs from being one of the most unpretentious punk veterans of the last quarter century out there. Hell, he may be the only one. . . .From adventures in little league to routinely getting pummeled by kids in suburban Greenwich and his own father, Tabb draws readers into his own existence, allowing all who dare a peek into his isolated, disturbing, hilarious and rebellious moments."—*Resonance*

"Tabb recounts his experiences with exploding crucified frogs, rapist dogs, homicidal turtles and astronaut hamsters. He pukes a lot, shits his pants on the Thunderbolt and is beaten up by what seems to be three-quarters of the population of Greenwich. . . . It's a fantasy many readers will recognize. Tabb's writing captures the spirit and mindset of childhood beautifully."—*The New York Press*

"*Playing Right Field: a Jew Grows in Greenwich* is my favorite Bookshelf review book of all time. . . . Tabb's comic timing is great: he knows when to pause and make you hold your breath for the punchline, and he always has a few surprises up his sleeve."—*Splendid*

"*Playing Right Field* is horrifying, hysterical, poignant and ultimately cathartic. It will speak to anyone who has ever felt ostracized for unconventional ideas or held to a different set of rules than the privileged class."—*Altar*

SURFING ARMAGEDDON

Surfing Armageddon

FISHNETS, FASCISTS AND BODY FLUIDS IN FLORIDA

By George Tabb

Soft Skull Press | 2006

Cover by Sarah Loukota

Published by Soft Skull Press
55 Washington Street, 804, Brooklyn, NY 11201

Distributed by Publishers Group West
1.800.788.3123 | www.pgw.com

Printed in Canada

Tabb, George.
Surfing Armageddon : a memoir / by George Tabb.
p. cm.
ISBN 1-932360-99-9 (alk. paper)
1. Tabb, George. 2. Punk rock musicians—United States—
Biography. I. Title.

ML419.T12A3 2005
782.42166'092—dc22

2005012964

For Nick

CONTENTS

GOIN' SOUTH

I HAD JUST FINISHED tenth grade at Greenwich High School, in New York City's richest suburb, when I found myself driving a motor vehicle for the second time in my life.

The first time had been about a week earlier, when I had driven my father's brand new Suburban to a local supply store to pick up some moving materials.

After my youngest brother Sam and I loaded up the mini-truck, the first thing I did was back the thing into a stonewall fence, probably built at least two hundred years earlier.

We both hopped out of my father's newest toy to survey the damage, and assess the beating I was bound to receive. But to our surprise, the only damage done was to the strewnabout stones. And a tiny scratch on the Suburban's trailer hitch.

Now, eight days later, as Sam sang along to "Sweet Transvestite" from *The Rocky Horror Picture Show* and "Sonic Reducer" by the Dead Boys on a cassette my mom and step-father, Nick, had made for us, I felt my father's brown and tan vehicle pull back and forth and from side to side along I-95.

South.

It wasn't like I hadn't felt it do that before.

The fact was, it had started doing that pulling thing about one minute after I had smashed down that rock wall. But I sure as shit wasn't saying anything, and Sam never even knew.

My father, Lester, upon driving the Suburban a couple of days after my "accident," felt the problem and brought it to the shop.

He was told the beast had a fractured A-frame.

Surprisingly, he blamed my stepmother, Cybill, who swore up and down she hadn't done it. But the two black eyes she received made her look mighty guilty.

*

As Sam, the Suburban, and I swung back and forth through the state of Delaware, so did the horses we were towing. Every few seconds I could see one or two of them stick their heads out of their tiny uncovered windows in the trailer behind us, and shoot me dirty looks. And Sassafras, our aging two-hundred-pound Great Dane, seated in the back seat, wasn't very happy either. She kept throwing up the kibble and canned meat she'd eaten for breakfast, so the car smelled like rotten dog food. And piss.

Our father, who had installed CB radios in all the Tabb vehicles traveling south demanded we not stop for hundreds of miles at a time. So I find myself trying to pee into coke bottles.

The first few times went okay, but while peeing to Susan Sarandon singing "Toucha Toucha Touch Me," I found myself getting excited, and my penis getting stuck in that tiny bottle opening.

"Take the wheel, Sam," I tell my brother, as we go seventy-five (at the slowest) trying to keep up with our stepmother the speed queen.

"I don't know how to drive," yells thirteen year old Sam, who takes the wheel anyway.

I try to pull the head of my penis out of the coke bottle, and the more I yank on it, the stiffer it becomes. It kind of feels good.

"Holy fuck," screams Sam, as a semi almost hits us from the right side.

I peer in the rearview mirror and now there are two horse heads, both with burning flames in their eyes, staring at me.

After an almost second crash with another semi, this time on the left, I grab the wheel back from Sam, and just let the coke bottle hang between my legs, swinging back and forth. I'm hoping it will fall off soon, and not caring about the piss that's going to spill all over the newly carpeted mini-truck.

"Breaker one-nine," I suddenly hear my father's voice yell as I finally gain some control of his stupid car and horses.

Sam, who had been attempting to yank the bottle off my groin, picks up the CB radio handset and tells my father, "Breaker one-nine, go ahead King Chief."

King Chief.

My father's chosen name for his CB "handle."

Ours was "Sweet Transvestite," which, of course, drove the rest of the family nuts. But I wouldn't answer to anything else.

"Breaker one-nine," my stepmother, Cybill, would say on channel nineteen, which we were all tuned into. "George, try and keep up, you little fuck."

Of course I'd ignore her and blast the tiny cassette player that was going through batteries we'd stolen from my dad's desk faster than Sassy could eat her vomit back up on the back seat.

"George," my sister Diana says, from our orange Datsun 510 wagon, that would later become mine through a series of unfortunate occurrences that started with a hot girl in short-shorts licking an ice-cream cone, "It's Diana, can you hear me?"

Sam gives up on my dick completely, picks up the handset and tells her of course we can.

I, of course, hit Sam. We only answer to Sweet Transvestite.

This was a tribute to our newest hero, Dr. Frank-N-Furter, from *The Rocky Horror Picture Show,* a movie my mom and Nick had taken us to see in the West Village, where it had started running at midnight only shows.

Of course we didn't understand much about the movie, but the one thing we did get was the naked girls. All over the place. On the screen and in the aisles of the theater. Changing from one outfit to another.

At first it felt like my mom and Nick had taken us to some porno show, where they were finally going to sell us into a child sex ring, like my stepmother and father had always promised they'd do.

But soon we began to really like the movie, and now, as we sang along with the Ampex cassette, we dreamed of wearing leather underwear and fishnets, never mind the high heels.

Yup. Healthy American boys.

"This is King Chief," we hear my father yell at us again, as we turn over the tape and listen to "Caught With the Meat in Your Mouth" by the Dead Boys, which is midway through the first album. Nick had found it at the New York Public Library on Tenth Street and Sixth Avenue and thought we'd like it. He was wrong. We loved it.

It was Sam's idea to turn the tape over.

He figured if I stopped hearing Ms. Sarandon's voice, maybe the bottle would fall off from between my legs.

When I heard the first electric notes ring out by Cheetah Chrome on "Caught With the Meat in Your Mouth," it not only fell to the floor and splashed us both in the eyes with our combined urine, it spilled all over the Rand McNally map my father had purchased for us, but which neither of us could understand.

"Okay," we finally hear my father's voice say over the CB radio on set to channel nineteen, "Sweet Transvestite, do you read me? Over."

I pick up the hand set with one hand, while putting my sore wiener back in my pants with the other.

Of course, we almost crash again. This time into a Clyde Brother's Circus truck. Which, in our twisted little minds, could have been funny. Dead clowns and tutued poodles strewn about I-95. Along with little people in their little cars. And lions. Lots of lions.

"Hail to the king," I finally say into the CB handset.

"Are you guys okay back there?" my father asks, as if he cares.

Which, actually, he does.

We're driving his new Suburban with the cracked A-frame, as well as some of his precious horses. It would be a sad waste to see those things go up in flames and smoke.

"We're fine," I lie to my father. "We just had a little trouble with a soda bottle. I got my dick caught in it."

"How many times have I told you not to lie?" yells King Chief through the tiny speaker.

I radio back that I can't hear him, then Cybill chimes in with "This is Queen Supreme" and asks if we can hear her.

I tell them both they are cutting out then quickly pull the power plug on the CB radio unit.

If they want me, they can come find me. I'll be the charred body on the left, right next to the tiny one on the right. In front of the canine corpse and two headless horses. Stupid fucks.

*

Obviously it wasn't my idea to move south.

It was all my father's.

Who had purchased custody of us boys years earlier.

If it had been up to me, I would have moved in with my mom and Nick in New York City, and spent night after night having fun. While I knew I'd be able to visit her during summer vacations and such, moving down the East Coast was my father's decision, and I had no choice but to follow.

After spending over a decade in the richest suburb of the United States, the old man finally decided that the land of white people with huge trimmed hedges just wasn't for him. Although he tried to fit in with the pasty faces and blue-eyed masses that infested the town, he was not allowed to join any of the town's country clubs because underneath it all, he knew the truth.

He was a Jew, like the rest of his family.

And Greenwich didn't like Jews.

And after years of being treated like he treated his kids, he'd had enough. So he decided it was time to leave pricey providence for some great expectations, for a place where he could start all over. A land where, like Greenwich, everyone would not be equal. A far off dream place where the four-teen point one million dollars he got for his cozy Greenwich abode got him one hundred and forty-nine acres of prime real estate and a mansion in the capital of not only Florida, but the entire Redneck Riviera.

Tallahassee.

His holy land. The one God had promised him as a small boy in Brooklyn, and had finally delivered. His Mecca, where he could and would be King Chief. Not because of the respect and humanity he showed others, but because he was rich. Filthy rich.

Even after buying the mansion and land, which, down South they call a "plantation," my father still had more money than anyone in southern Georgia and northern Florida.

Which, of course, isn't saying a lot. But it spoke volumes about his character.

My father moved me, my two younger brothers, Luke and Sam, as well as my two stepsisters, Diana and Teresa, and half-sister, Stephanie, to the land of eternal sunshine. And while Cybill bitched about it for months and months, when she discovered slow-drawling "southern gentleman" and the overwhelmingly cheap price of labor, willing to do anything, she was whistling Dixie in no time.

*

Eventually the entire family did reach my father's promised land. And in almost one piece, too.

Turns out one of our cats, Monster Pussy 2, who was riding in one of the horse trailers, decided to off itself by jumping into freeway traffic rather than face looming unknown called the "Deep South."

And when my beloved Great Dane Sassafras, or Sassy, discovered this new hellhole *was* home, she intentionally walked into an oncoming semi on Route 319.

To this day, I envy her courage. I wish I had had the guts to follow.

In a way, I eventually did.

BLITZKRIEG BOP

SO THERE I WAS, back in New York City, after a few weeks in the bowels of the Redneck Riviera when I saw them come onto the tiny stage at CBGB.

It wasn't like I really knew who they were, with their black leather motorcycle jackets, soup bowl haircuts, and heavy Queens New York accents. I was at this scary club with the most disgusting bathroom in the world an hour after meeting my old pals from Greenwich, Chris and Nikhil, at Grand Central Station.

We were going out and getting drunk for the night because we knew in the city they served underage kids, and they *never* asked for an ID.

Which was a shame, because our fake ones looked so real.

Anyway, after taking my two pals to *The Rocky Horror Picture Show*, and busting their cherries, so to speak, we were well on way to CBGB. Still virgins in real life. But eventually, things would change.

*

"Did you turn gay when you moved to Florida?" asked Chris, on the cab ride to the diviest bar on the Bowery.

"Huh?" I ask him, confused.

"That movie was the fuckin' faggiest thing I've ever seen," he tells me in his thick French accent.

"Yeah," says Nikhil, an Indian from India.

That's what he always told us when he asked him where he was from.

I was "George the Jew," Chris was "Chris the Frog," and Nikhil was "Nikhil, the Indian from India."

We had more than enough black eyes and bloody noses to prove it.

"You are gay, aren't you," exclaims Chris. "I always knew it. It's cool your Mom and stepfather Nick let you out of your closet!"

I could have told them I wasn't really into men, and that the joys of masturbation had just been bestowed upon me as a strange gift from my father the cross-dresser, but I let it slide. We were almost to the club, and if they wanted to think I had sex with men it was fine with me. At least they thought I was having sex, which, at that point in my life, is really all that mattered.

*

"Tip the man," Nikhil yells at me, as I'm the last one out of the cab at the corner of Bleecker and Bowery.

I tell the guy my tip is to check out *The Rocky Horror Picture Show*, he'll see lots of naked women in the aisles, and then he just smiles back me with an almost toothless grin.

"Tank you, sir," he tells me, meaning it.

As we enter the graffiti covered club, which wasn't really that graffiti covered yet, we feel the stench of dog shit and stale beer work its way up or noses. Mine and Chris' first, since ours are the biggest.

"It stinks in here," I tell the bearded biker at the door, who charges us each around four bucks, a lot of dough in those days.

"Uh huh," says the smelly Hell's Angel-looking guy who takes our money, then goes back to reading a copy of the *Village Voice*. The newspaper that's the bible of what's going on in New York. Where we'd read about this band, the Ramones, that was to perform that night.

I'd been to the club after *Rocky Horror* before, but this was the first time the place was packed. The bar was three people deep, and it was hard to see the stage off to the right of the club.

"Is this band supposed to be any good, fag?" asks Chris, and we let Nikhil fight his way through the crowd for some bottles of beer.

I tell him I hear they are pretty rockin', like that band Kiss and Thin Lizzy, which is what all us "freaks" listened to in the tenth grade. I also told him I thought they were a gang of angry Puerto Ricans.

"You were a freak," Chris reminds me, as we both stand there in our Izod shirts, "Nikhil and I were normal."

"Yeah, whatever," I tell my still preppy friend.

"A freak, and now a fag," Chris says to me. "What's next, you going to run away and join the circus to fuck elephants? I hear wonders about their long trunks!"

I try to ignore the guy who used to tell me in tenth grade that he liked to eat out women with a spoon. That he loved drinking "pussy juice," and a tablespoonful was just enough, while a teaspoon was too little.

I had no fucking clue what he was babbling about, and felt sorry for any cat that got in his way.

He also taught me those five magic French words that got me knocked on my ass by this beautiful French girl named Monique, who rode on our bus to high school everyday.

She hopped onto the bus in super-tight jeans and a warm fuzzy pink sweater that made my heart ache.

"Go ahead and say it," Chris prodded me, as he stepped on the school bus after her.

Nikhil smiled.

We'd all met on this bus a few weeks earlier, and I think I thought I was in love.

"What were the words again?" I ask Chris as he took a seat next to me.

"Stop being a dirty Jew and just walk up and say it," Chris yelled at me.

So I did.

I walked up to the prettiest girl on the bus, and spit out those five French words.

"Te shat, me fe bonde."

At first Monique just stared at me with those wide open beautiful brown eyes.

"She likes me," I thought to myself.

Then the next thing I know I'm sitting on the slotted and rubberized soaking wet floor of the school bus.

Monique is standing over me with her biology and math books, with my blood on their back covers.

"You creep," she yells at me, then kicks me in the cheek, "go back and tell my fucking brother he's dead. I'm telling Mom!"

I'm not sure if I was in shock, or awe, as I crawled my way back to Chris and Nikhil.

They were laughing, of course. But at least Nikhil had a *slight* look of guilt on his face.

"Ha ha you dumb Jew," laughed Chris.

"What's wrong with "I think I love you?" I said, feeling the warm fluid on my head make its way down toward my eyebrows.

Both guys laughed some more, but eventually, their humor wore off when they realized I needed stitches.

*

So, there we are, all drinking the imported beer Nikhil purchased, when they walk onto the stage.

At first I think they're either a platoon of hippie soldiers or superheroes that dress almost as cool as the Fantastic Four.

The bass player and guitarist plug in, make some noise, then the thin-as-a-rail singer says, "Hey, we're the Ramones and this one's called 'Rockaway Beach'".

"One-two-tree-fo," the bass player spits out, and twenty minutes later, we find ourselves still standing in the same spots, not having had one sip during their entire set.

Finally, able to speak, and be heard, I say to my Greenwich pals, "Did you see that?"

Their looks of amazement and unmoving lips tell me everything I need to know.

*

Later that evening, as we all lay on my Mom and Nick's floor in their apartment on West Fourth Street, we keep talking about *that* band. How they played so fast, and didn't ever stop. Not even once.

When Chris tries to turn the subject to me being a homo for taking them to *The Rocky Horror Picture Show*, Nikhil ignores him, and just keeps saying how loud and cool the band at CBGB was.

Of course, I agree.

*

A couple of weeks later I found myself packing up to return to Tallahassee and start the eleventh grade. It had been a wonderful month of *Rocky Horror*, french fries, and coffee every day with my Mom at a village restaurant called Sandolinos. And it was my first exposure to a live band that didn't play disco like the Village People that I actually liked.

Of course I couldn't remember their name, and upon arriving back down South after paying in cash my mom gave me for my flight on People's Express, it all just became a drunken blur.

A blur that would some day come back into focus and change my life.

Forever.

RECONSTRUCTING TARA

"YOU'RE THE JEWS," exclaims my friend, and only friend, Tracy, "and you live on Water Oak Plantation."

"Ssssh," I tell my pal with a girl's name. "Don't tell anyone!"

"You're the rich Jews. The ones on the cover of the *Tallahassee Democrat!*" exclaims Tracy from the back of our remedial English class. It was held in some dumpy trailer that Leon High School calls "the new wing," but which is in reality just another parking lot.

"Please," I say to the kid with the Confederate flag on the front of his cap, "keep it quiet!"

But of course, he can't. He's never seen a Jew before. Never mind one that lives on a plantation.

An hour later, the news seeps into the brain of every kid in the school, and by the end of the day, I find myself, a whiffle ball bat, and the entire football team alone in the gym.

But let me back up a bit.

*

Once my dad closed the deal on the plantation, he moved his family of six kids, two adults, and one housekeeper into a two bedroom apartment on Killarn Way. A nice suburban street where we were supposed to play baseball and ride bikes with the other kids until our new "home" was complete.

Of course none of the other kids would have anything to do with us, and once, at the bus stop, I ask why.

"Cause you're Yankees," says one toothless kid with long hair and a John Deere hat, "and we don't like Yankees down here!"

"The South will rise again," another kid suddenly shouts, and all of a sudden, it's Greenwich all over again.

Fists are flying, and lips and noses are bleeding.

When I try and ask these kids in blue jeans and cowboy boots why they are kicking my ass, all I keep hearing is, "You damn Yankee."

Now, I have to be honest here.

I am a Yankee.

Or at least, I love them.

Been a big fan since 1972, when Thurman Munson, the catcher of the team, signed a ball for me before telling me it took my mom nine months to take a shit.

I had no clue what he was talking about, but after I got that ball, I continued to yell "bozo" at him like all the other kids, and had his Topps card from every year.

Later, I would see my favorite team win like three years in a row, and actually attend a couple of World Series games.

But somehow, I think something was lost in translation.

*

After about a week of getting my ass kicked at the Killarn Way bus stop, I finally ask some girl named Bobby Sue, a boy's name, what was with all this "Yankee" stuff.

She slowly explains to me that the term "Yankee" meant "Northerner" down here in the Redneck Riviera.

That is a term lower than "nigger," who she explains, were put here on God's green earth to serve the white race.

Having no fucking clue what she is talking about, I ask her why all this hatred?

"It's not hate," she slowly explains, pronouncing every word strangely. "It's love. For God, *and* his mistakes!"

She then explains that black people were nothing more than apes that could talk.

"Like in *Planet of the Apes*?" I asked her, "Or *Beneath the Planet of the Apes*? Or *Escape From Planet of the Apes*?"

She just stares at me, with her head tilted, like a dumb dog.

Then she speaks. "You really are a stupid Yankee, aren't you?"

*

On the bus that sunny day, Bobby Sue explains to me the social ladder as she understands it. The lowest are the blacks, which, of course, she calls "niggers." Then there are "Yankees," which she tells me I was because I helped free "the niggers," putting an end to their free labor.

When I try to explain to her that that happened way before any of us were born, and what's wrong with black people working for a living, anyway, she tells me that at the top of the social and evolutionary scale are white people.

Christian white people.

"What about Jews?" I ask her.

"What's that?" she asks, in all seriousness.

"I dunno," I lie. "I just heard that word before."

"Oh," she says, then pulls out a six inch switchblade and stabs the green school bus seat in front of us.

The knife goes all the way through and almost stabs the kid in front of us.

"What you do that fo'?" asks the kid as he turns and glares at me and Norman Bates' kid sister.

"'Cause I don't like niggers," she calmly replies.

It's then I realize I *am* in Hell.

*

After a few months sleeping next to my stepsister, Diana, who is twelve days younger than me, I get tired of waking up with a hard-on in the family living room on the pullout couch, and ask my father when we'll be able to move to our new house.

"Soon, Son," he tells me.

"What's the holdup?" I ask.

"Those damn retarded kids," he tells me.

When I ask him what he's talking about, I get his side of the story.

*

It turns out my father purchased the property of Water Oak Plantation on Route 319 on the northern border of Florida from the state. They were selling the land cheap because it housed a large building called "The Florida Sunshine Home for the Retarded Children," or something very close.

And my father liked cheap.

But, as it turns out, he didn't like the retarded.

Especially the kids who currently lived on the property.

Short of putting them all in a room together, and burning it down, my father believed enforced sterilization was the right answer.

For anyone he didn't like.

He figured that these retarded kids should never have been born. Plus they were getting in the way of his dream.

When I asked him what dream, that's when things got really weird.

*

"I want to rebuild Tara," my father tells me as I lay on the pullout bed, browsing the most current issue of *MAD* magazine I have.

"Tara?" I ask, "What's that?"

"You don't know what Tara is?" my father yells.

Then he punches me in the face.

Hard.

"What'd you do that for?" I ask him, tears running from my eyes.

Emotionally, it really didn't hurt anymore. I'd cut myself away from that bastard years earlier. So I wondered why I was crying.

Physical pain?

"I punched you 'cause I got a dumb ass nebbish for a son," is his reply.

Then he goes on to tell me about Tara.

"Son," he says, like he didn't just give me a right hook to the face, "Tara was the mansion in *Gone With the Wind*."

I knew better than to ask what *Gone With the Wind* was. So I just listened.

"*Gone With the Wind*," he continues, "was the greatest film ever made next to *How to Succeed in Business Without Even Trying*. Later they made it into a book."

"A book?" I ask, astounded that my father reads anything besides literature about the Third Reich.

"Yes," he explains. "In the movie and in the book, a man builds his dream house down South. A southern mansion. Where he lives happily ever after."

"Okay," I say, tears, blood, and snot drying up.

"Here," my father says, and with that, goes over to the shelf of books in the living room and shows me the cover of a hardback book that looks like it's never been opened.

In the picture on the cover are two old movie stars I recognize, and behind them, a giant white mansion with four big white columns and everything.

The man and woman are kissing, and around them are horses, and acres of beautiful land.

"That's me and your sister," my father tells me.

"Huh?" I say.

"Your mother. That's me and your mother," my father stutters.

"Lovely," I say.

Of course this time it was a left hook.

"Anyway," my dad explains through more blood, snot, and tears, "I'm rebuilding that house as almost an exact replica. I'm gonna get some slaves and everything."

I look at my insane father, and wonder if this time he's really lost it for good.

"We're gonna have lots of land for us to ride our horses on. Attie, our housekeeper, can now be promoted. And best of all, you boys are going to learn to be men."

"Men?" I whine, deep in my heart knowing I'll die a virgin and always be a boy.

"Yup," my father says, "in fact, tomorrow you start work on the property."

"Work," I moan, hating that four letter word.

"Yeah," explains my father, "I finally worked out a deal with some schmucks at the state capitol, and they're going to rid us of those annoying unwanted guests."

"Oh," is all I can muster up, and the next day I find myself, along with my brother Sam, starting demolition work on the mental institution, to rebuild my father's version of Heaven.

And that day, as we started work, I wished I were Gone with the wind.

*

"First you knock down the sheetrock," explains Laurie Mozier, a man with a girl's name, as Sam and I watch.

Laurie picks up a sledgehammer and bashes a hole in a wall of the master bedroom on the second floor, complete with porch and balcony.

"I wanna try," exclaims Sam. He grabs the sledgehammer away from the college aged kid and tries to break a hole in the wall.

But the only thing he almost ends up breaking is my foot.

He drops the sledgehammer less than two inches from my fake Converse high-tops I purchased last year at Woolworth's for under five bucks.

"Better let George try it," laughs Laurie.

I pick up the heavy beast of a tool and pretend that one of the walls in the room is my father. I hit it so hard the metal part of the tool breaks off and flies forward into the next room, where a hole is born.

And it feels good.

"Jesus, George," Laurie exclaims. "Take it easy."

I tell him I will, and ask if he minds me drawing pictures on the walls before I destroy them.

He tells me since it's all going to the dump, I can do whatever I want, and that he'll even pay me a dollar an hour because it looks like I work hard.

He explains my father hired his company, Mad Dog Construction, to redo the place, and although I was not to be paid, Laurie thought I should be. So there I had it. My first job in the Sunshine State.

*

A week later I found myself having drawn fifty pictures of my father with charcoal on many of Tara's walls. They all had huge holes in them, and many were missing their heads.

Eventually, after learning how to correctly use a wheelbarrow, I was able to cart the destruction out to a waiting dumpster.

This went on for months.

Every day after school in the first months of the eleventh grade, I found myself knocking down walls.

Well, that, and jerking off.

I'd figured out how to "rub myself the right way" a few months earlier, and now, I was getting lots of practice. But we'll get to that later.

In the meantime, I'd carry folded up *Playboy* centerfolds in my jeans pockets, hang them on walls, and wank into piles of dust. I figure I must have masturbated at least five times an afternoon.

And only got caught twice by my boss.

The first time he saw it was the picture of the beautiful strawberry blonde, who was 5'3", as tall as me, but much older. At least twenty.

As I looked at her posing with her panties pulled down around her knees, and read that she thinks "Nice guys are a turn on," I came into a pile of broken sheetrock on the floor.

"You are going to shovel that up?" asked Laurie, who startled me from behind.

Embarrassed beyond words, I put my penis away and just nodded my head.

"Good," laughed Laurie, "and forget *Playboy*, I'll bring you something better tomorrow!"

From then on in it was Penthouse Pets. And the second time I get caught with the meat in my hands, Laurie told me even though I beat off a lot, I was still his fastest worker, so he wouldn't dock my pay. He just wondered how I could do it so fast.

"Practice," I told him. "Practice."

*

Eventually, my father's dream of his house from *Gone With the Wind* came to fruition. With all the walls knocked out, and cum stains removed, the place became almost livable.

That is, until the day Sam and I almost burned it down.

We were told to light a pile of wood and debris on fire.

And burn it.

When we asked my father what we should use to ignite it, he gave us a can of gasoline, then made his way off to the barn he was having built to house his antique cars and stable of stallions.

So Sam and I did what we were told. We poured a bit of the fluid on some wood and lit it. It would burn for about three seconds, then go out.

So eventually we got the idea to just start a *little* fire, then pour the can of gasoline directly on the damn thing.

After a loud whooshing sound, I found myself driving my little brother to the emergency room, while he screamed in pain and stared at the skin falling off his palm onto the car seat.

I had driven over to the barn to ask my father to drive us, because, truthfully, I was really shaken up, never mind the fact I had no eyebrows and could hardly see.

"It's your fault, George," my father told me, "so you take care of it."

"It" of course, being my little brother.

After a while, his hand did heal, but not before Lester, my father, put him back to work shoveling horse shit with a blister covered hand.

When Sam complained of pain, my father just said, "Use the other hand."

I wasn't sure about Sam, but I knew I couldn't live without my right one.

*

A few weeks later I find myself in the Leon High School gymnasium, hitting a whiffle ball to my only friend, Tracy.

He swears up and down he didn't tell anyone that I was the kid who lived in that house on the cover of the local paper, but the football team hitting their fists into their hands on the other end of the court tells a different story.

"Tracy," I say, "why?"

He and his Confederate flag hat tell me he only told one person. The captain of the cheerleading squad, named Laurie.

Who just happened to date the football team's captain.

"Gotta go," Tracy quickly says, seeing the angry mob approaching, and he hauls ass out of the gym.

So it's me.

Alone.

Against an entire team of huge guys.

"Jew, Jew, Jew," they start chanting.

Old familiar feelings wash over me like a huge wave.

"Jew, Jew, Jew," they continue as they get closer and closer.

I raise the whiffle ball bat in self-defense, knowing it's useless and I'm done for.

Suddenly, one guy on the team runs ahead of the pack and grabs me.

He holds my arms behind my back, and the rest of the team approach me.

"So you're the Jew," says the captain, whose name, believe it or not, is Biff.

I say nothing.

"I hear you are filthy rich, gimme some money," he demands.

I tell him I have none, that my father's a cheap fuck, and to leave me alone.

A couple of the guys rustle through my pockets and find my wallet. And all of the dollar and thirty-five cents I've saved up.

"This won't do," snarls Biff. "Take him to the locker room."

*

As they carry me toward that stinky room full of jock sweat, I try to wiggle my way loose.

No luck.

"Jew, Jew, Jew," the football team starts to chant again.

They finally get me into the locker room and stand me on my feet in the shower room with twelve nozzle heads.

"It's time," says Biff.

Time for what, I have no idea, but being around that many people in a small room with all those shower heads makes me more than a bit uncomfortable.

Then everyone gets quiet.

So quiet we can hear a toilet flush in the girl's locker room next door.

"Well?" asks Biff.

"Well, what?" I say, knowing I'm about to have the entire football team end my life one way or another within the next couple of minutes, and at this point, not really caring.

"You know," says Biff.

"I know what?" I yell at the team's captain, "I know you're gonna kill me? I know you're gonna stomp all over me? Well go ahead. Take my life, please."

Everyone laughs.

Except me.

"Drop 'em," yells Biff.

"Huh," I ask the jock in the team jersey with the number thirty-three on it, with his slicked back blonde hair and tight fitting blue jeans and *new* sneakers. Damn him.

"Drop your pants," Biff explains.

Visions of prison rape race through my mind. Here I am, alone with the school's football team, and they're gonna have their way with me. Not that there's anything wrong with that, except I was not going to consent.

"Drop your jeans," Biff yells again, this time, with his fists squeezed into big balls of hate.

I start to think of what my friend Chris from Greenwich had told me over the summer a few months back. That I was a fag. A homo. And now I wished it were true.

"I'm going to ask you one more time, Jew," snarls Biff.

So I do what I'm told.

I undo my belt, unbutton my jeans, and pull down my pants and underwear.

Of course I'm so terrified my balls are the size of marbles, and my penis tries to hide back in its shell like those small green turtles you buy at pet stores that always die within a few weeks.

Everyone is quiet.

We hear another flush coming from the girls room, and I start to hope that they just kill me when it's all over.

Suddenly, through the corner of my eye, I see one of the team's players approach me from the left.

He leans down in front of my penis.

Everyone remains quiet.

Then he speaks.

"It's true," he says.

Suddenly every guy on the team is fighting for a spot in front of me to get a good look at my dick.

"It really is missing the skin," Biff exclaims.

"It is!" exclaim the others.

They tell me to make it a bit bigger so they can get a better view. So with wiener in hand, I try my hardest.

And little by little, it grows.

Everyone oohs and aahs.

Then gives me a round of applause.

Finally Biff speaks. "Ya know," he says, scratching his head, "I hear chicks dig that sort of thing, did it hurt when they cut you?"

Speechless, I just stand there like an idiot.

With my dick in my hand.

"Really," says Biff, "when they took away that skin, it must have hurt, huh?"

Finally beginning to realize I'm not gonna be raped, I start to come out of my fear induced coma.

"Well?" asks Biff.

I tell him, and the rest of his team, that it didn't hurt all that much, but what did was the bionic arm they put on my left shoulder.

I explained that although I wasn't the Six Million Dollar Man, because I only had one bionic part, it did do a lot of damage.

"Huh?" says some team member.

"Yeah," I explain, "most Jews get them when they're thirteen. It's some rite of passage bullshit. Your dick gets cut and you get the arm."

*

The next day at school, Biff sees me in the hallway near my locker and, while looking at his feet, walks up to me.

"George," he says, with his heavy southern accent, "about yesterday . . ."

"What do *you* want?" I yell at the jerk.

"Nothing, dude," he quietly says, "nothing at all."

"So?" I say to him.

"Well," explains Biff, "my girlfriend likes you. You can date her if you want to. Please just don't beat me up."

I tell him I won't, as long as he behaves himself, and eventually I end up taking him up on his offer.

Which is when things got even weirder.

ALL THAT JAZZ

SO THERE I AM, having the same dream for the third night in a row from my comfy bed in the northern wing of Water Oak Plantation.

It involves me, my penis, and that Tallahassee Mall on North Monroe across the street from where they showed *The Rocky Horror Picture Show*.

In my dream, I'm running past all these stores inside the artificially lit George Romero death trap.

I see my brother, Luke, working as usual, over at Orange Julius. I see my other brother, Sam, getting his glasses fixed for the fifth time that week because my father once again broke them with his fist. I see my stepmother, Cybill, naked and playing with a horse's penis in JC Penney. I see my stack of sticky *Penthouse* magazines, which were supposed to be near my bed, now being sold in some cigar shop by one of my best pals, Louis.

And I'm pissed.

But what really bothers me is the money in the fountain.

It's not only a waste, it's a downright nightmare.

As I stare at the pennies' shiny reflections, which burn halos upon my irises, I think about the starving children in Africa. Or the ones in my house.

Then I see it.

The Easter Bunny.

All pink and fluffy, and really soft. The ears gently slice the air above its head, and its tail has never been rounder or firmer.

I feel my penis get so rigid that if I walked into a wall, I'd still break my nose. But no matter. There was no denying it. The Easter Bunny was hot, and for some reason, I want to have sex with it. Like a rabbit.

As I approach it to stroke its now wet pink fur, since it was playfully swimming among the lost coins and water in the cascading fountain, I hear it speak in a gentle woman's voice.

"George," it says seductively, "George . . ."

"George," the voice continues, making my dick so hard it could hold up a wheelbarrow full of porn, "George, wake up."

I open my eyes in our family's newly finished mansion designed after Tara in *Gone With the Wind*, and see my sisters Stephanie and Teresa.

Their faces are beet red and they can't help but giggle.

At first I'm not sure where I am, then, what they're laughing at.

One look down toward my feet and the answer awkwardly pops up.

The blanket over me not only looks like a tent, but one of those ones they use in the circus. It's huge. There could easily be lions, tigers, and bears beneath the big top.

An Easter Bunny or two, as well.

I quickly yell at my little sisters to get the fuck out of my room before I tell my Dad or Stepmother, and they laugh and giggle and point at my circus pole pecker as they leave my room early that school morning.

How embarrassing.

Not that my sisters saw one of those painful erections that I woke up with every morning. That, I couldn't help.

But I was dreaming of having sex with the Easter Bunny.

My worst fears had taken a turn south.

Not only did I think I might be gay every once in a while, because of those thoughts of Tim Curry as Dr. Frank-N-Furter in those hot fishnet stockings, but now I was getting excited by the thoughts of animals.

What was next, sheep?

Ewe.

*

My fascination with the Easter Bunny had begun several weeks earlier.

One day, after spending a few hours after school helping my father build fences across our sprawling green land of sunshine and depression, my dad asked for a favor.

"George," he said in that tone that meant "peasant," "I need you to go to Sears and pick up some more studs so we can build this here fence straight across Oklahoma!"

"Huh?" I say to my father, not knowing what a stud was, but knowing his fantasy of being a cowboy in Oklahoma had not only gone to his head, but to my hands, as well.

"Go get some fucking metal studs at Sears you little piece of shit," my father replied, in a rather nice tone.

For him.

"Okay," I said, running off, leaving my tools behind, happy to get away from that maniac, who had now taken to wearing white suits and white hats, and who practiced cracking a bullwhip in the barn every night.

"And don't forget to put away your tools," he shouted after me.

I pretended not to hear him as I started his Chevy Suburban and hauled ass down our driveway as fast as I could.

On the way to the mall, I only almost ran into three trees, one kid with a backpack, and someone's house.

The damn car pulled to the left.

Gee, I wonder what that could be about.

*

"Can I help you, sir?" asks the pimply faced kid behind the tool counter in the back of the overly lit Sears-Roebuck.

I felt bad for him. He too had a shitty job, and his pimples were almost as bad as mine. Worse, truthfully.

I only had a few, but they were big motherfuckers, the underground kind. The ones that hurt your face before they even start to swell under your skin.

The kind that once it began to surface, you would wait a few days, then take a pin, pop a hole in its center in front of a mirror, then watch in amazement as you'd squeeze it so hard that the white pus would shoot further than the Clorox-smelling projectile stuff from your penis ever did.

And it was harder to clean as well. You really need a sponge and some Windex to get that crap off of the mirror. And god forbid if you did it in your car.

The only answer I could ever give when that happened and someone saw the goo was "I picked my nose and had no where to put it."

Anyway, I explained to the kid, who must have been all of one year younger than me, that I needed those metal thingies that help keep fences together.

He asks me what kind and I tell him I don't know.

So he pulls out a huge box of shiny metal objects and has me point to the ones that look familiar.

I do, then get the hell outta that store.

I was still pissed about the place ever since my father had gotten me that lawn mower a few years earlier.

*

As I walk through the mall, stopping in briefly to check out Spencer's Gifts—well, the tiny sex toys, and the hot posters of babes in the back—I wonder why my brain is so fucked up.

As I left Spencer's, seriously looking forward to the day I would turn eighteen so I could buy a shotgun and splatter my brains all over the hills of Water Oak Plantation, I was shaken from my thoughts by It.

The Easter Bunny.

Although it is more of the winter holiday season, what with the mall Santa feeling up small children around the corner, I take it the Easter Bunny is working for another gift shop doing some sort of promotion for colored Christmas eggs.

I guess this because the bunny was standing next to a sign on an easel that reads, Christmas Eggs, and stands between myself, the Easter Bunny, and that fountain with all those shiny nickels, which reflected the joy of the season upon my scorched blue retinas.

"Wow," I think to myself, "that Easter Bunny is hot."

Of course, suddenly finding myself excited for someone in a fluffy outfit, I am now more sure than ever there is a Heaven and a Hell, and my path was leading directly past Heaven.

"Hi," the Easter Bunny says to me, shocking me out of my fantasies.

"Uh, hi," I kinda mumble back to the Easter Bunny, quickly glancing about to make sure no one sees me talking to what could very easily be that invisible rabbit in the old Jimmy Stewart movie.

"You're kinda cute, you know," says the Easter Bunny, with the softest and fluffiest voice I've ever heard.

I look into its white eyes with the black marbles rolling around in the plastic bubbles, and instantly fall in love.

"Are you okay?" asks the Easter Bunny, after I stand, staring at it for easily over a minute while saying nothing.

"Yeah," I finally spit out. "I'm sorry, I don't know what to say!"

"Tell me I'm cute," says the Easter Bunny.

Not only do I tell it that, I tell it I love its color, its tight round tail, and its long stroke-able ears.

The bunny laughs in that cute Easter Bunny sort of way.

Finally, getting up the nerve to ask the big question, I begin to spit it out.

"Easter Bunny," I say, in all seriousness, "I was thinking and . . ."

"Of course I'd love to go out with you!" exclaims the giant rabbit, and with that, runs over to Santa Claus and his elves to tell him the good news.

The little boy that was on Santa's lap is brushed aside as the hot ass Easter Bunny takes his place.

I wait until the rabbit is done talking to Santa to get some information, but they just keep yapping and yapping.

Suddenly, from all the nervousness, I feel a bout of diarrhea hit me like my stepmother's wooden spoon, and the next thing I know I'm in the mall bathroom, my ass making all sorts of sounds I've never heard before.

As I'm sitting there, wishing the pissing out of my ass would stop, I look at the roll of toilet paper to make sure there's enough to clean up what is going to be a huge mess.

Then, I sit back so hard in shock I dent my back from the toilet pipes.

Near the full roll of paper is an eye.

A human eye.

Looking at me.

Through a hole in the wall.

Then it asks if I want to plug up the hole with anything.

I quickly grab one of the fence studs, and ram it in there.

A half hour later, while still searching for my lost Easter Bunny, I see an ambulance arrive and wheel off some middle-aged, overweight guy who seems to be bleeding from one eye and moaning in pain.

Whatever.

I'm pissed as hell. The Easter Bunny is nowhere to be found, and now I have no idea to find it.

And waiting until April was not an option.

So I find my brother Luke at Orange Julius.

Well, find him in the back of the place, smoking a doobie.

"Did you see where the giant Easter Bunny went," I desperately ask my brother.

"Huh," says Luke, as he inhales another stiff hit from his hand rolled joint.

"The giant Easter Bunny," I repeat.

My brother hands me the joint and tells me I need it more than he does.

And, for once, I don't argue.

*

A few days later at school I'm bitching to my friends Louis and Scott how I met the perfect Easter Bunny, but have no clue who she is.

When Louis, the smart-ass he thinks he is, with his thick brown framed glasses and curly brown Italian hair and pimple covered face asks me how I know it's a girl, I explain that I've never heard a voice softer and sweeter.

"Happy Birthday Mr. President," replies Scott, who with his balding blonde head, is both shorter and more blind than myself. His wire rim frames hold coke bottle thick lenses, and his voice sounds almost the same as the Easter Bunny's.

"Cut that out," I yell at my pal, who has promised that once he graduates from school this year, he'll let me have sex with his girlfriend, Cindy, so I can lose my virginity.

Hell, just kissing a girl would be a thrill for me.

I hear you can use your tongue.

Anyway, as Scott, Louis, and I argue about whether the Easter Bunny is a man or a woman, or an invisible figment of my demented imagination, Mr. Bott, our psych teacher, interrupts us.

"What's going on guys?" asks the grizzly young looking guy with the beard and the body that made all the cheerleaders in our class sit up front in their tiny outfits with their legs spread wide open.

"George wants to bone a bunny," says Scott, laughing, as Louis, who is turning purple from laughter at this point, falls on the floor clutching his stomach.

"I do not!" I yell out, but Mr. Bott, the all knowing cool dude who read each and every one of the journal entries he made me keep in the eleventh grade and gave me A+++++'s on each one, knew the truth. He'd read it.

"Why not just ask around who she is?" asks Mr. Bott, "Someone around this place must know!"

I tell him in a quiet voice that maybe, just maybe, it's a guy, and that would suck.

"Who cares," Mr. Bott and his hippie long brown hair tells me. "Emotions are emotions. If they feel good, they are good. For your heart. And for your soul."

I loved that guy.

*

Two days later, after asking everyone in school if they knew about the talking Easter Bunny at Tallahassee Mall, now I'm not only known as the "Circumscribed Yankee Jew," but one that's a pervert, too.

Scott tells me it's called "bestiality," but it doesn't count if you do it with your own dog.

He then explains about how to put peanut butter on your wang, and have the family dog lick it off.

"It feels so good," explains Louis, who's listening in on our conversation.

"Tell me about it," replies Scott.

"Yeah," says this girl, Laurie, who unknown to us, is standing behind Louis, Scott, and myself in her cheerleader outfit, complete with the L on the front for Laurie, I guess.

She's the captain.

I guess that's why everyone else has an L, too.

Anyway, we're shocked.

This was a private conversation between three guys about man's best friend.

And Scott tells her so.

"I've heard crazier stuff," she says, in a soft and pretty voice.

I then look at her closely for the first time.

Her eyes are bluer than the most beautiful sky I've ever seen, and her flowing red hair reminds me of a gentle breeze on a California beach at sunset.

Her smile is what I like the best. It makes my heart flutter and feel funny, and suddenly I find myself unable to speak.

"Umm," I stammer, but it's hopeless.

"George is really shy," says Louis, "so ignore him. Tell me about the crazier stuff!"

Suddenly, I'm furious. I don't want to hear this beautiful woman to talk about stuff she shouldn't. She was a true beauty. A goddess. And goddesses are as pure as the driven snow. What ever that means.

"Don't say anything," I manage to spit out. "I like you!"

Scott and Louis stare at me in amazement.

Laurie stares at me with puppy dog eyes.

And I can't believe I just said the L word.

*

The end of that week found me having a date with Laurie.

My first date.

Not only with her, the captain of the cheerleading squad, but, like, my *first* date.

Ever.

I was so nervous that I kept asking my dad if I could borrow his pickup truck and after telling me "yes" five times he just took to hitting me. Which I understood better anyway.

On the way over to her house that night, as I drove my father's stick shift beast with the stainless steel welded in bed, I straightened out my clip-on tie and looked at my face over and over in the truck's rear view mirror.

When I got near Laurie's house, about seven miles from mine, I parked around the corner and did what I had to so I wouldn't walk through her door and start humping her leg like our housekeeper's little poodle, Peachie, used to do to us all the time.

When I was done, I wiped up the mess with the "I Love The Sunshine State" green tractor cap my father kept in his glove compartment and walked around the corner to meet the love of my life.

*

"You must be George," Laurie's father says to me after I ring the door bell and some old guy answers the door.

"You must be Mr. Williams," I say to the gentleman, who is dressed in a jacket and tie like myself. "It's nice to meet you."

I stick out my hand, and he sticks out his. We shake like real adults and everything.

"Laurie has told me lots about you," says Mr. Williams, then shouts upstairs, "Laurie, honey, your little friend is here!"

Little?

So what if I'm 5'3" and weigh just over a hundred pounds. I'd just reached puberty, what did he expect? Plus, one day I knew I was going to have a growth spurt. It was just taking its sweet fucking time.

"Tell him I'll be right down," says Laurie, in that soft and beautiful voice again. I feel goose bumps rise all over my body.

"So, George," says Mr. Williams, "I hear you've been accepted into Harvard and Yale. I'm a Yale man myself."

I just nod my head, not believing the line of bullshit I fed Laurie she not only believed, but told to her dad.

Suddenly, Laurie's mother walks into the room. She's almost as beautiful as her daughter, just an older model. Her eyes too are blue, and hair, flame red. The only real difference I can see between the two are the breasts.

Her mom's are huge!

"You must be George," says Mrs. Williams.

I reach out, grab her hand, and kiss it.

Like real adults do.

And Dr. Frank-N-Furter.

"Enchanté," I say, not knowing what it means, but knowing it seemed to work on Janet in *The Rocky Horror Picture Show.*

"You're lovely," says Mrs. Williams, as her skin turns the color of her hair. "Laurie has only told us good things about you."

"Phew," I say out loud, by mistake.

"Is there something we should know?" asks Mrs. Williams, now concerned.

"No, don't be silly," I say, waving my hand as though there's nothing crazy about me to possibly know.

"I'm so glad you have chosen an Ivy League school for your higher education George," says Mr. Williams, "Laurie's boyfriend, Biff—"

"Hush up," Mrs. Williams suddenly interrupts.

"Laurie's *ex*-boyfriend, Biff," explains Mr. Williams, "has only very simple ambitions. After high school, he wants to go from being the captain of the football team to simply being a coach."

I'm not sure what I say next as I'm busy adding two plus two up in my head. Laurie is Biff's girlfriend. Biff is the guy who almost gang-raped me in the boy's shower at Leon High School, but instead was impressed with my sculpted sausage. And all of this added up to nothing good.

"Biff has even told us about you," Mrs. Williams says. "He says you are a very kind and smart gentleman."

I tell her Biff's right, and what a great guy he is.

They both smile and tell me that even though I'm a Yankee, I'll fit in fine in Tallahassee if I keep up the good attitude. And grades.

"Anyway," continues Mr. Williams, as I hear Laurie stumble around upstairs for makeup and whatever else girls do to prepare for dates, "I am seriously hoping you lean toward Yale, I know some people up there and—"

"Hush up," Mrs. Williams says again, looking directly into her husband's eyes. "Let the boy decide what's best for himself!"

"Right," says Mr. Williams, who then asks, "Where are you taking my daughter tonight?"

I tell them I know of a wonderful French restaurant nearby, and about the movie, *All That Jazz*, that's playing at the Tallahassee Mall.

"Laurie loved seeing you there," explains Mrs. Williams, "although she says she's not sure you recognized her in that silly Easter rabbit costume of hers."

I tell her of course I did as my mind goes into total shock.

What happens next, I don't remember.

All I do recall is that Laurie came down the stairs looking more beautiful and redder than ever. She took me by the hand and told her parents we'd be home by eleven or something. I must have said stuff, but only remember drooling once we got into my dad's truck.

And thinking about her as the Easter Bunny.

*

Of course the French restaurant was an Italian one, where my friend Louis worked. He served us a quiet romantic French dinner of spaghetti and meat sauce, explaining to Laurie it was the hit of good old gay Paree.

Impressed, Laurie told me that it was true that my friends were smarter than hers, and she was so glad to be on a date with "a true gentleman."

As we finished our meal, I noticed that she really was redder than ever. I asked her about it and she explained that she had been at the beach all afternoon, and was completely sunburnt. And that it hurt.

I felt my heart sink.

*

All That Jazz, the flick about Bob Fosse, that dancer and writer guy of Broadway, starred that Amity Police Chief named Martin Brody in *Jaws*. This movie, however, had no sharks eating anyone, but was both emotionally stirring and intellectually stimulating.

Which meant, of course, Laurie didn't understand a thing.

After the movie she kept asking me questions about why a man who was supposed to be dying was singing and dancing. That he should be in a hospital, or better yet, in church, praying for God's forgiveness. For sleeping with men. Like she suspected Louis and Scott did.

Dumbfounded, I didn't answer any of her questions but instead asked her about her sunburn as we drove back to her home in my dad's truck.

"It really hurts, but not enough, I don't think!" she exclaimed.

"Enough?" I ask her.

"Yeah, *enough*, silly," was her reply as she looked me directly in the eyes.

In the reflections of her beautiful eyes I saw myself, a seventeen-year-old kid, who still knew nothing about women, except that a man plants a seed inside a woman and then that seed grows and she has a baby. I'd seen that in one of those cutout Time-Life books my stepmother and father had got for us kids when we were in grade school.

"Well," says Laurie, then closes her eyes and puts her mouth near mine as I park in front of her house.

I panic. I'm not sure what I'm supposed to do. Do I kiss her? What if it hurts her sunburn?

Do I reach over and touch her breasts? Will that hurt as well? Isn't that a rude thing to do?

Finally I do what I think is right and grab her hand and shake it.

"It was great seeing you tonight," I say, feeling like the biggest pussy in the world, but afraid of doing the wrong thing.

"That's it?" she asks.

"What's it?" I reply, in all seriousness.

"Jesus, George," says Laurie, in a voice very much *not* like the Easter Bunny, "I had plans for you."

"You did?" I ask, stunned.

"Yeah," she tells me as she starts to slip some tinfoil covered Alka-Seltzer or something back in her purse, "You were going to go to Yale, get rich, and I would get to live out my life's dream!"

"Which is?" I ask, hoping like hell I can still make whatever wish she has come true.

"Well it doesn't matter, obviously you're gay like Scott and Louis," she screams at me as she starts to leave the truck.

"I have to know," I say to her, looking in those once beautiful blue eyes that now burned a mean purple.

"Okay," she says, then tells me.

"My plan was to marry a rich guy, then spend my life laying around in bed having sex and watching soap operas all day," she explains. "Could you even imagine a better life than that?"

On the way home I realize I can't.

*

Years later I heard the Easter Bunny married the High School Coach.

And part of her dream must have come true. They sure did have a lot of little bunnies running around.

LIVE AND LET DIE

SO, THERE I AM.

Dead.

My heart has slowed down to the point where I can see the bright light at the end of the tunnel.

I can hear that whooshing sound as I start to zoom backwards away from my lifeless body, which lays next to the horse trailer I'm supposed to be hitching my dad's pickup truck to.

As I feel my soul tugging against death, I notice a stain on my white Izod shirt from the drool that I haven't been able to stop for the last hour.

It's on my blue corduroy pants as well.

"Great," I figure, I'm dying dirty.

They'll probably remember me as a hippie since my brown hair is long and curly, worn up in a Jew 'fro.

And they'll probably bury me in the next twenty-four hours.

I hear they do that with Jews. Bury them in a plain wooden box as fast as possible.

I'm almost wishing I could wait around to see if my dad shills out the bucks for wood, or goes with cardboard, which is much more his style.

As the tugging gets harder, the white light, closer, the feeling of knowing this would happen is hitting me hard.

I always knew I was going to die young. I just didn't think it would happen this soon.

And what's worse is that I'm still a virgin.

And I *knew* I'd die a virgin.

Knowing I'd kissed one girl, Denise, about a week earlier, just isn't enough. I'm seventeen, and about to reach the pearly gates where I'm sure to be laughed away.

"You can't come in here," that Gabriel dude will say. "You're not a man yet!"

Others will laugh around me and point. Especially at the tiny mound of pubic hair I wished so hard into existence.

Then they'll tell me to take the elevator.

South.

"Just push H," they'll laugh.

And what's killing me—no, make that killed me—is I knew it. I fucking knew it. My life had been a total waste so far, and that is how its going to end.

I'm pissed.

But let me back up a bit.

*

I'd met Denise about seven days before in the parking lot of Leon High School, in Tallahassee, Florida.

It was my junior year, and she, who had big boobies and the biggest lips I'd ever seen, had taken a liking to me.

Why?

I have no clue.

But she kept telling me I was cute, and she dug guys from New York.

Then she introduced me to her "best friend," Robert.

I could tell they were sort of dating, as I'd seen them holding hands in the hallways near my locker and stuff, but I didn't want to say anything.

"This is Robert," says Denise to me that sunny Florida afternoon in late autumn, "and he has something I think you'll like!"

As I look at Robert, with his long straight brown hair, buttoned down snakeskin shirt, and pointy cowboy boots, I wish I could be one zillionth as cool as this guy.

"Hi, George," Jim Morrison Junior says to me. "Denise has told me lots about you!"

"She has?" I say, surprised.

Nobody I knew talked about me. Unless they were saying I was either a Jew or gay. Or both.

"Yeah," continues Robert, "she tells me you really dig *The Rocky Horror Picture Show* and that you've seen it plenty of times in New York."

I tell him that that's true.

"She also tells me you were able to convince a local theater to play it here on midnight every weekend, as well," he adds.

I confess that I am indeed a nerd-freak, and that seeing that movie twice a week is as close to salvation as I'll ever get.

It was like church to me.

Definitely a religious service.

"Guess what Robert has?" says Denise with her long blonde hair in her hippie dress, as she shocks me out of my thoughts.

I wanted to say "a big dick." But I didn't need to get beat up again that day.

"What?" I ask the both of them.

Richard then pulls out a sandwich bag full of hand-rolled cigarettes.

"You know what these are?" he asks.

"Duh," I tell him, "those are hand-rolled cigarettes like my baseball coach used to smoke. And like the ones they smoke in the aisles of the Waverly Theater in New York during *The Rocky Horror Picture Show*."

Robert looks at Denise, confused.

"Smell them," Denise finally says, after a long and awkward silence that left me slightly confused.

Robert opens the bag and I take a deep whiff.

"Yup," I say, "just like the kind Coach Andrews used to have."

"And the kind they smoke at *Rocky Horror*?" asks Robert.

I tell him "Yup!"

Suddenly they both break out in laughter, so I do as well. I'm really not sure what's so funny, but whatever it is, I want in.

As we continue to giggle, that stench of horse manure continues to sting my nose from those funny hand rolled cigarettes.

Finally, as the laughing subsides, Denise explains to me that these cigarettes are rolled up pot.

"Pot?" I ask.

"You do know what pot is?" she says, accusingly.

I tell her of course I do, but what did cooking tools have to do with smoking?

"It's Mary Jane," says Robert, to clarify things.

"Like those little candy things?" I ask, clueless.

"It's grass," Denise says.

"Oh," I say, sighing, "the stuff my dad makes me cut every weekend. I didn't know you could smoke it."

"It's a special grass," explains Robert. "Wanna try some?"

I answer sure, why not, and follow them to Robert's shiny black pickup truck in the lower Leon High School parking lot.

We get into his overly huge truck cab and Robert asks Denise and I what we want to listen to.

I whip out the Dead Boys' *Young, Loud & Snotty* tape I got from my stepdad, Nick, and tell Robert to put it on his Archer brand stereo system.

He does and it's blasts away the tune "High Tension Wire."

"Whoa," I say, pushing the stop and rewind buttons, "you have to hear it from the beginning."

"Cool," say Robert and Denise in unison, and then take out some funny looking dried weeds from the truck's glove compartment, and stuff some into a funny little pipe.

My life was about to change.

Forever.

*

Ever since I was about six, my father, Lester, and stepmom, Cybill, always told me if I continued to be the awful human being I was, I'd end up a drug addict.

Later, like after a whole year, they began to tell me that my mother and Nick, who lived in New York City, were not only drug addicts, but drug dealers as well. They threatened me that if I was ever really bad, they'd send me to live with them where I'd be sold into a white child slavery ring.

I had no clue what the hell they were talking about, but it certainly did scare me.

As the years went by, my father and stepmom accused me of being on "drugs," whatever that meant, at different stages of my development. I remember once Cybill telling me that I smoked marijuana, and that was why I was so short, and was never going to reach puberty. Another time she told me that my smoking marijuana was making me stupid in school. Even another time, she told my guidance counselors in junior high I was on the stuff, and I had to take some sort of detention class with a bunch of really scary kids.

But the truth was, I never even tried the stuff.

Nor saw it.

I wasn't interested. The only drugs I took were the ones that promised to clear up the zits on my face, but never did. Oh, and aspirin, for the all the bruises.

*

As the opening riff of "Sonic Reducer" by the Dead Boys blasts loudly in the black cab of Robert's pickup truck, Denise hands me the funny little metal pipe and she tells me to inhale.

Deeply.

I do.

Then almost vomit.

The smoke tastes sweet, yet stings the shit out of my nose.

Robert tells me to take another "hit" and I do.

I figure, what the fuck. My parents always accuse me of taking drugs, so why not try them?

Again, I cough out a large cloud of sweet smelling smoke, and spit all over the tinted windshield.

"Once more," says Denise.

Not wanting to be a pussy, I inhale as deep as I can and hold it in.

Tightly.

As the stereo blares those magical guitar notes from Cheetah Chrome, the whooshing sound in the song suddenly jumps to the forefront. Then, to my amazement, out of the stereo and onto my lap.

It looks like one of those wave machines you can buy at the mall, only this one is made of air, and the flowing liquid is gray and white.

I finally exhale and Stiv Bators' voice beings to sing "I don't need anyone" and I realize, that in the cab with Robert, Denise, and I, are two stick figure people, who are dancing along to the Dead Boys on Robert's dashboard.

I say "hi" to them, and they wave back.

Cool.

"So what do you think?" asks Robert as he takes a deep puff, then hands the now slithering metal pipe to Denise where she sucks on its shiny head with the forked tongue that keeps poking in and out, making me laugh uncontrollably.

"More," is all I can move my mouth to say, and again they give me the snakepipe.

I inhale deeply, as I watch the little stick figure people dance around, and feel a door swing open in my brain. One that I never knew existed, but one that led to mysterious and wonderful things.

Needless to say, the rest of that morning, and day, is spent getting to know my new best friend, Mary Jane.

We hang out between classes, and by the time the final bell rings, I'm begging Robert for some more.

He tells me to come to Denise's house that night.

*

When I finally find her house on some road with lots of trailers, I see Robert and Denise standing on what looks like a concrete porch, but upon closer inspection, is just some cement blocks holding up a huge piece of wood.

"Fuck you, Denise," yells Robert as I approach, full of smiles and dreams of seeing those little stick people again, the ones who had told me some great jokes earlier that afternoon. But for some strange reason, they made no sense when I tried to figure them out later.

Anyway, as I get closer I hear Denise talking in an angry and low voice to Robert.

"I can fuck whoever I want," she tells him. "You are *not* my boyfriend, a boyfriend wouldn't sleep with a girl's mother."

"I couldn't help it," explains Robert. "She asked me to and how could I say no?"

"Some fucking eighteenth birthday present you've given me," Denise screams, then kicks him in his ass. Hard.

"Fuck you, bitch," yells Robert, as he starts walking toward me.

Wow, I thought, they talk just like my parents.

"Are you guys okay?" I ask, as I near Robert, who is about to walk through me like I'm not there.

"You can have her, George," says Robert. "She's more stuck up than a tampon."

I'm about to ask him what a tampon is, but before I know it, he's in his truck and is driving away.

On the cement block porch, Denise just stands there, tears rolling down her cheeks.

*

Ten minutes later I find myself in the basement of Denise's family's dwelling unit. Whatever it is.

We are sitting on the couch, and she's telling me that "that fucker" Robert had sex with her mom.

Having seen her mom when I first entered the house, watching *That's Incredible* on the television, I didn't blame the guy.

Like Denise, she had long blonde hair, and those same pouty lips.

Only when *she* talked, her voice sounded like a frog who had swallowed too much gravel and sand.

Anyway, I'm sitting next to Denise in her tight blue jeans and blue sweater on a brown plaid couch, and she's going on about how she turned eighteen today, and this was the present he gave her.

As she talks and talks, I start to feel anger well up inside of me. Not only is Jim Morrison Jr. not a virgin, he's done it with at least two women, has the coolest truck, and a pocket and glove compartment full of the most magic plant I've ever inhaled.

"That guy sucks," I finally tell Denise, when I've heard enough. "He doesn't know how good he has it!"

Suddenly, her face turns from a frown to a smile, and she looks me directly in my blue eyes. Hers are green, and I can see her pupils begin to enlarge at a freaky speed.

"You really think so?" she asks me, as her left hand touches my right.

I stare into her eyes and suddenly decide I'm in love.

Not only is this woman beautiful, she's as delicate as a flower, and her scents are pure ecstasy.

"I—" I begin to mumble.

"Ssssh," says Denise, and with that, puts her mouth over mine and suddenly I find my tongue doing the tango, box-step, and hustle, all for the first time.

And it's wonderful.

Really wonderful.

It certainly felt better than anything I'd ever experienced before, even the door that swung open in my brain earlier that afternoon.

As we continue to kiss, I feel Denise's hands touch my chest.

And that feels good.

No, make that great.

It's like suddenly I'm not just one person. There's someone else there with me, inside me, and for the first time, ever, I don't feel alone.

Tears of joy begin to roll down my cheek, and that stops Denise's tongue and hand right away.

"What's wrong, honey?" she asks me.

"Nothing," I sob, wondering what the fuck is wrong with me, then realizing someone actually called me honey besides my real mother.

"You need to relax, sweetheart," coos Denise, then takes out a hand rolled cigarette from under the couch cushion, and lights it up for me to smoke.

"Toke it," she tells me.

"Huh?" I say, my brain still in shock from hearing the word "sweetheart."

"Inhale," Denise says softly, and I do.

Suddenly, that door swings open again, and on the couch's armrest behind Denise, I see those little stick figures again.

They are both smiling with huge grins, and applauding me.

I smile back at them and give them the thumbs up signal.

"Are you the Fonz or something," laughs Denise.

I tell her that, yeah, I am that cool.

I must be really stoned.

"Good," Denise says softly. "Because I want you to give me a special present for my birthday."

What she wants, I'm not sure at all, but I smile at her again, and suddenly our tongues are once again intertwined.

*

As we kiss each other with all our strength, Denise moves me until I suddenly I find myself laying on top of her on the brown plaid couch.

We kiss heavily, and every once in awhile Denise whispers "breathe" to me.

After what seems like hours of joy, but was probably only minutes, I look up and see the two stick figures with question marks above their heads.

I try to will them into saying something, but all I can hear is my heavy breathing.

And Denise's.

So we make out some more and I feel Denise's hand make its way down my back and firmly grab my butt.

It feels so wonderful I yelp, and more tears start to flow.

"Are you okay?" she asks between kisses.

I tell her I'm fine, and she takes my right hand and slides it between her legs.

Over her tight jeans I feel a wet warmth like nothing I've ever touched before.

It feels soft, yet hard against the denim.

I give it a little squeeze, and Denise moans.

Loud.

I jump off of her, and start to apologize right away.

"I'm so sorry," I say to the love of my life. "I didn't mean to hurt you. I really didn't."

Then, like the pussy I am, I start to cry.

Denise softly takes my left arm and puts it around her shoulder, then leans me into her breasts while I quietly sob.

"It's okay, honey," she keeps saying over and over again.

But it isn't.

I hurt her.

I don't know what to do, because no one ever told me, and now I've destroyed the best thing I ever had.

"It'll be fine," coos Denise, and my tears eventually slow down as my snot drips on her pretty blue sweater.

The fact that my head is on her boobies doesn't even hit me until days later. And even then, the shame and guilt I feel make me try and try to erase the whole memory.

*

Fifteen minutes later I find myself standing with Denise on her plywood and cement block porch, as she inhales deeply from her Marlboro cigarette.

"Are you smoking again, Denise?" I hear her mother's gravely voice croak from inside the house/trailer/whatever.

"Yes mother," replies Denise, who is then told by her mother that next time she goes to the store, to get her a pack of smokes as well.

"I'm really sorry, Denise," I start to tell the blonde-haired beauty, but she puts her index finger to my lips.

"It's okay, George, it's really okay sweetheart."

I feel goosebumps all over my skin.

"I understand," Denise continues, "you've never done this before. And that's something special. Something I'll *never* take away from you."

I don't know whether to kiss her feet for being the greatest person on the planet, or break her fucking skull open, because, well, this was just further proof I'd die a virgin.

In the end, we just slowly kissed, and I think I told her I loved her.

*

A couple of days later at Leon High School, I found myself alone again with Denise and Robert in his truck, smoking "doobies," a term Robert had taught me.

It seems that Denise and Robert had made up that night after I left, and while my heart still pounded deeply for Denise, never mind my stiff crotch, it was slowly dawning on me that we were all just destined to be friends.

Which was okay.

Because Robert had great pot.

As we smoked and smoked, I turned Denise and Robert on to this other record Nick had found for me at the New York Public Library, and recorded on an Apex tape.

It was by a band called the Ramones, and it was simply called *Ramones*.

The songs were short and fast, and I wasn't really sure if I liked them or not, but they sure as hell sounded familiar.

Especially the "one-two-three-fo" part.

A few months later, after seeing *Rock 'n' Roll High School*, I remembered.

But for the time being, I just really dug the chainsaw guitar sound, and this one tune called "Today Your Love, Tomorrow The World." It mentioned Shock Troopers and the Fatherland, so I knew it must be about Star Wars.

As the guitars blasted from the right speaker, and the bass, from the left, we kept saying "whoa" to one another and laughing.

As did the stick figures, who were now dancing on the rearview mirror, and giving each other high-fives.

I liked those little guys.

But what happened next I kind of blame on them.

*

The next morning in the parking lot of Leon High School, I find Robert and Denise in the truck, all bummed out.

"What's wrong?" I ask the two of them, while Robert sits with his arms crossed, and Denise sits on her hands.

"Stairway to Heaven" is blasting on the stereo.

"Robert's stash got stolen," Denise tells me, furious.

"Stash?" I ask, not knowing shit about what it meant.

"Yeah," says Robert, "some fucker broke into my truck and stole not only all my weed, but the money I was making with it as well."

"I told you you shouldn't have left it in here," screams Denise.

Robert just tells her to pipe down.

I mention that I guess there goes my pot for the day.

"Listen, George," says Robert, "there's this guy, Kevin Forrest, and he deals."

I look at him blankly and wonder why he is telling me about a guy who likes to play poker.

"Anyway, you can find him after school, at three PM, in the upper parking lot. He's got thick, wire rimmed glasses, and is as skinny as a pole. Tell him I sent you and it's for me."

"What's for you?" I asked Robert, who shot a glance at me like I was really stupid, which I was.

"The joint," Robert explains. "Tell him you want to buy a joint for me, then you can have it."

"Oh," I said to Robert, "But why should I tell him it's for you?"

"'Cause we're going down to Miami now to get some more shit off the boats," Denise says, "and he won't sell to anyone unless there's some connection."

It turns out I should have taken that long ride with them.

Or better yet, just ignored their advice.

*

At three PM sharp that afternoon, I find Kevin Forrest out in the parking lot where they said he'd be.

I walk up to him and breathe deeply. This is my first drug deal. I know if I get caught I'll probably spend the rest of my life behind bars, instead of losing my virginity like I hoped.

I'm so nervous sweat is dripping into my eyes.

I, of course, realize that could also be from the fucking Florida humidity, which rusts cars faster than Robert's glove compartment gets broken into.

"What's up?" says the skinny, nervous looking kid with the owl like wire rimmed glasses after I circle him about seven times.

"You Kevin?" I ask, trying to sound all tough like I see the guys on *Starsky & Hutch* or *Baretta* act.

"Who's asking?" is his reply.

I think of sticking out my hand and introducing myself, and being the nice guy I am. But this guy sells drugs. From what I understood about these sorts of people from the television, as well as from my father and stepmother, is they'd shoot you just for looking at them wrong.

And they're also gay, addicted to heroin, and come from families who raise their children in cages, or worse, horse stalls.

Anyway, I tell Kevin Forrest that Robert "sent me for his stuff."

He grabs a cigar box he's got clutched under his right arm and opens it.

Inside I see tons of Marijuana cigarettes, as well as some loose stuff packed tightly into wads of cellophane.

Wow.

"Robert, huh," says Kevin, with a sort of weird smile. "Well, okay then."

He sifts through all these joints that look exactly the same and pulls one out with a small "R" hand written in pencil at the thing's tip.

"Here ya go, that will be one dollar, sir!" he explains.

I give him the buck, put the thing in my pocket, hop on the school bus, and make my way home, hoping like hell the police don't find me.

Obviously, they don't.

*

The next morning at six AM, I wake up bright eyed and bushy tailed. I'd hidden that joint in my James Bond tarot card reading game. Actually, they were real tarot cards, and I, by that time, had learned to read both the major and minor arcana. I was pretty good at telling people's futures. Including mine, which always came up as "death."

After taking a blazingly quick shower and using Irish Spring soap, and smelling it every two seconds to wake up, like on the commercials, I get dressed in my only Izod shirt from Greenwich still in one piece as well a blue pair of corduroys.

On my feet I wear my cheap Woolworth sneakers with the holes in the bottom that I had taped up with duct tape. My friend Burke had turned me on to it at school.

I have a quick breakfast of Lucky Charms, as I watch my brothers and sisters fend for themselves.

That's the way things work over at Water Oak Plantation. First come, first found.

All the food is fair game for everyone except the stuff in the tupperware marked either For The Girls or Dad's.

It feels so nice to be loved.

Anyway, after Luke finishes his Coco Puffs, and Diana a yogurt, we all start to make the one mile hike to our bus stop at the end of our driveway.

I tell my other two siblings to walk ahead of me, and when they do, I whip out that joint from its hiding place in the James Bond game that I'd shoved in my pocket.

Then I light it.

With a pack of matches I stole from my father's office desk, where he kept his pipe collection, the one Cybill always bitched about and constantly threatened to sell. The one my father would slap her around about, and scream at her that if she ever touched them, she'd have it worse than me.

Which, of course, was probably already the case.

*

The first match goes out from a cool breeze that morning, but the second one takes well, and the glowing ember begins to shine brightly as I inhale as deeply as I can.

With one toke, I manage to smoke almost half the thing.

The penciled in R is long gone.

After exhaling, I feel that door swing open, and there, on the driveway, in front of me, are those two little stick figure guys. Today they are wearing white Izod shirts and blue cords like mine.

Which surprises me.

They're usually naked.

Just sticks and circles.

Anyway, one of them waves frantically at me, crossing his arms in front of his body over and over.

The other guy just has that stupid question mark above his head.

So I take another puff, and another, and another.

It's sure going to be fun to get on that school bus Luke calls the "Nairobi Express" for reasons I don't understand until many years later.

I figure that I'll be so stoned I won't care if the other kids make fun of me and call me "rich" and "Jew" and even try to untie my shoes. I have my boys with me.

The stick figure duo.

They'll somehow make it funny, so I can laugh it off.

After one last puff, I snub the end of the joint into our driveway, and put the "roach" into my pocket.

I learned that term from Robert as well.

I figure there might be a little left, and maybe I can smoke it after school.

That is the last clear thought I have before I die.

*

As I approach our bus stop I know something is wrong.

Not only does that one door swing open, now ten of them do.

Not only that, everything starts to change color and suddenly the sky is purple, the grass, black, and Diana and Luke, neon pink.

This is fucked up.

Then I see police lights.

At first, thousands of them.

Then, millions.

It's like I'm watching the opening credits of *The Mod Squad*, only I'm in it.

This isn't right.

"Are you okay?" asks Diana in a voice so low and slow, I wonder if she really is Satan's daughter.

"Yeah?" asks Luke, from high above me as I feel myself slowly sinking into the pavement on our driveway.

"I'm drowning," I tell them, and they both just laugh.

But not me.

I'm scared shitless.

The driveway is eating me up, and I can't swim through hard surfaces.

"Something's very wrong," I tell them the both of them. "I smoked a joint a few minutes ago and I think I was poisoned!"

"You too?" says Luke, with a smile that stretches from ear to ear.

Then around the back of his head.

Diana says nothing.

"Seriously," I say, as my lungs tighten up from the cement now flowing through my chest, "someone is trying to kill me. I think I smoked rat poison."

Turns out I'm underestimating, but we'll get to that.

"No one wants to kill you, George," says my brother Luke. "Just relax and go with the flow. And what the hell are you doing drugs for, anyway. You're already nuts."

Diana puts her arm around me and somehow pulls me out of the concrete quicksand. I thank her for saving my life as I wipe the dust from my knees.

"I better go home and tell Dad and Mom," I say to her and Luke. "If I get on the bus, I might die!"

Diana offers to walk me back the mile up the driveway but I tell her I'll be fine.

Even though I'm quite sure I won't be.

As I start to walk away from them at the corner of Water Oak Plantation Road and Route 319, I see myself watching as the bus stops to pick them up.

*

The next thing I know I'm following myself up a grassy hill that keeps turning from black to white.

"This is fucked up," I hear myself say, and nod in agreement.

Once I conquer one hill, I take on another, then another.

I try to run, but the faster I go, the more I lose my will to move.

So I take it slow.

One step at a time.

It seems to take forever as I become bored watching me in that white Izod shirt and blue corduroys float over the now gray and white grass toward the mansion.

Eventually I do reach it, but by then, everything has turned into a cartoon.

A scary one.

A really fucking scary one.

*

I walk in the side entrance of the house into our kitchen, and find Cybill, with my younger sisters, Stephanie and Teresa.

Cybill yells something at me, but I can't hear her because I'm too far away from my body, and hers.

So I move in closer.

"What's wrong with you?" I hear her ask me, and watch as I try to explain that I've been poisoned.

"What the hell are you talking about?" Cybill laughs, then my sisters join her.

The laughing becomes so loud I watch myself plug up my ears, then move away from the action because it's annoying.

"You do know you're going to die," I hear a voice behind me and myself say.

I look back without turning my head and see the two stick figure guys. The one who who had a question mark over his head now has a pair of X's for eyes, and is hanging from a children's drawing of that game, Hang Man.

"I'm going to die?" I ask the other stick figure who was waving to me off a short while earlier. He's now is sobbing.

"You're not going to die," sneers Cybill to my body, which catches all of our attentions.

"Yeah, you are," says the stick figure, as I watch him pull a stick hanker chief from his stick pocket, and wipe his round face.

"Yes I am," I see myself tell Cybill. "I smoked some pot, and it was mixed with rat poison or something."

"I knew you were on drugs," Cybill yells, scaring the pants off the dead stick figure who's just hanging around.

I watch myself explain to her that today was only like the fifth time I ever tried the stuff, and the first time I ever bought it.

Of course, she doesn't believe a word I say, nor do I, or the stick figures. We all sit back and laugh.

"You probably just smoked some very strong hashish," Cybill told my body, "or some good pot. And pot's not for pussies."

Teresa and Stephanie laugh as my cartoon father floats into the kitchen, demanding to know what's going on.

We all watch as Cybill explains to her husband that she always knew her stepson was a drug addict, and now she had proof.

The stick figure guy who was dead cuts himself down from his stick rope, and clutching the other stick figure, laughs so hard they both fell forward onto my body's shoulder.

"Get off of me," I watch myself say, and with that, watch in awe as my father slugs my body's face in the mouth.

"Don't talk like that to your mother," he says, and I must admit, I find myself laughing along with my pals. This cartoon is insane.

*

What seems like hours later, my father walks me, my body, and my two stick pals outside into the bright sunshine.

As we leave the house, I can see the ants on the stairs in front of us as close to my eyes as Denise was the other night.

I can see every hair on the ants' faces, those beady black eyes, and those pincher things that could crush my neck.

So I scream.

Me and the guys have a real yuck fest about that one.

We also giggle as we watch me tell my father that I can hear every thunderous step they take.

"George, my idiot son," my father tells me, "you must have just smoked some bad pot. For some reason, I feel sorry for you, but I'm not sure why."

"Why?" laughs one of the little stick figures.

The other one laughs as well.

But I find myself crying.

And my body, too.

My father takes my arm and walks me down our cartoon driveway to the barn, where he tells me he's going to put me to work until the drug wears off.

I watch myself keep insisting I'm going to die, but he just laughs, and tells me he'll kick my ass tomorrow, when I'll remember it.

Now that is funny.

And me and the stick figures laugh until our sides hurt.

*

Eventually, my father puts me to work attaching a horse trailer containing two scary beasts and flies the size of baseballs to his truck.

The harder I try to move, the faster I become paralyzed.

Then everything breaks down.

On an atomic scale.

At least, that's what the stick figures tell me.

They explain that the world is made up of tiny molecules, which are really just a bunch of atoms. Nature's building blocks. The molecules combine to become different things.

Like metal or wood.

And even people.

But now it is all disbanding in front of our eyes.

Like when you look really closely at a comic book picture.

Everything is just dots.

And that is happening all around us. The world, my universe, is decentralizing.

That's when I feel my heart start to slow down way too much.

I watch as I clutch my chest and gasp for air.

Me and the stick figures float higher in the air to find my father, and eventually find him off in a field about a quarter of a mile away.

Too far to float to.

So all we can do is watch me die.

*

As we hover above my lifeless body, which is now limp and laying in a bed of dust near the horse trailer, I suddenly feel someone grab me hard from behind.

"What the fuck?" I scream, though my body does nothing. Not even move its lips.

"It's time," one of the little stick figure guys says to me, and although I don't want to admit it, I know damn well what he's talking about.

Suddenly I feel myself flying backwards toward the sky, and a very bright light.

As I draw nearer, I hear familiar voices from when I was a kid, and I can almost make out some faces.

"It's all gonna be fine, George," says the other stick figure, suddenly as tall as I am, as he wraps his arms around me.

They feel comforting.

And warm.

Then we see my father enter the picture.

It's hard to see him standing next to me through the bright lights shining behind us, but we watch as he starts to hit my body's chest and do CPR.

Then everything goes black, and I wake up in the back of an ambulance.

Alive.

*

Three days later Kevin Forrest is introduced to my Louisville Slugger with the Reggie Jackson autograph, and they become so close they're like blood brothers.

I tell Robert and Denise what happened, and they ask if I still have that joint.

I tell them I do, and they say bring it to a lab, but don't use my name.

I get a better idea, and give it to Dr. Kennedy, the shrink my father has me seeing after school.

He's really nice, and keeps telling me I'm the "intended" patient, and that my father is the one who's really nuts. And that I should really go live with my mom.

Fearing white slavery and heroin dealers, I tell him I just can't.

Anyway, I give Dr. K. the roach, and come back a week later to a rather pale headshrinker.

"Where'd you get that pot?" is the first thing Dr. Kennedy says to me when I walk into his office.

I explain, like last week, that some kid named Kevin Forrest sold it to me, but I took care of him.

"Well," says Dr. Kennedy in all seriousness, "we ran some lab tests but I didn't tell them where I got it because it would have involved the police."

"The cops care about rat poison and pot?" I ask.

"There was a little pot," explains Dr. K, "but mostly we found PCP, LSD, DDT, and some really strong hashish."

"Damn," I cursed under my breath. That bitch was right.

"We also found some other chemical compounds used in elephant tranquilizers, as well as cyanide."

I sit there looking at him and his balding head.

Speechless.

"What I'm trying to tell you, George, is that joint was meant to kill someone."

I leave his office speechless, and tell Robert about it the next day at school. I even remember to tell him about the little pencil marked "R" on the joint, and then Robert tells me he's gonna have a word with Kevin.

After that day, I never saw either of them again.

*

A few months later I try pot again and start to trip and think I'm going to die right away. I have mean flashbacks, and swear off the stuff forever.

I tell this to my father who insists we go see my shrink together since I mentioned the words "intended patient."

My dad walks into the guy's office at the onset of our appointment and screams and yells at Dr. Kennedy that he's a useless piece of shit, and shouldn't be practicing medicine.

Dr. Kennedy tries to calm down my father, but my dad gets even more enraged and turns over the old guy's desk and threatens to kill him.

At that point I really wish I could smoke just one little bit of marijuana.

Because I really want those stick figure guys around to see this.

They'd love it.

HE'S A LADY

"FRANK-N-FURTER, it's all over, your mission is a failure, your lifestyle too extreme," I sing as I stand in front of the packed AMC movie theater a few weeks after giving and getting my first French kiss.

I'm in a gold lamé outfit.

Borrowed, of course.

With a blonde wig and banana on my head, a metal detector turned ray gun in my hands, and *The Rocky Horror Picture Show* flickering on the screen behind me.

"I'm your new commander, you know I'm a prisoner," I continue, while looking at my friend Tammy, who is wearing a French maid's outfit. We are facing an audience full of jocks, rednecks, drama students, and unbelievably, my father.

"We return to Transylvania, prepare the transit beam," I sing.

"Wait," shouts Courtney, the hottest girl I know, even though she likes to dress as a man, "I can explain!"

I stand there, gawking at her, in her black wig, black lipstick, black eyeliner, black sequined pumps, black fishnets, black corset, black cape, and black underwear with a bulge in it.

I was in love once again.

And things were about to get really weird.

On a night.

A night I'd never forget.

*

It was one of those cool autumn evenings and my junior year of high school in Tallahassee, Florida. Which, if you're from anywhere else in this country, is equivalent to the sixth grade.

Tops.

Anyway, to stay away from my father, I had taken a full time job after school at a local supermarket called Publix. Where I was gainfully employed as a bag boy. Along with my pal, Louis, and his wavy brown hair, pimple covered face, and owl rimmed glasses.

While he never stopped bragging that he was a senior, and I was just a peon junior, I saw right through him. We were both the same. Pussies.

We'd decided to become bag boys together because we heard cashiers put out.

Whatever that meant.

And on weekends, life was all about *The Rocky Horror Picture Show*.

*

"No George," explains Henry, the local Publix floor manager, "how many times do I have to tell you, it's cans first, then the bread."

I look at Henry and just shrug my shoulders.

I knew that cans go first, followed by other heavy stuff like powders and hard cookies, then the lighter stuff, but I liked to fuck up people's food.

It was one of the only small pleasures I had.

Aside from masturbating five times a day.

Besides, the lady I was bagging for never, ever, tipped me, and would make me load up her bags into the back of her pickup, which had a very nasty dog in it, who always tried to bite off my huge Jewish nose.

"Ya got it, George?" asks Henry, with his usual slur.

I tell him I do.

I kind of feel sorry for Henry. He is at least fifty years old, and his big job in life is watching a bunch of us little jerks bag groceries for his neighbors.

Actually, Henry used to have another job, but he lost it.

Due to an accident.

He at one time was a vet. But now, all he had was a horse-shoe shaped dent permanently imprinted on his forehead.

Our stock boy pal, Tommy Corn, had told us this. He said Henry was behind a huge horse trying to give it an enema.

"Get back to work there, young man," yells Henry, shaking me free from my thoughts. "And you may make stock boy one day like Tommy. That's if ya keep at it!"

With that he walks over to me and pats me on the shoulder.

I start to feel really bad for him.

"Stock boy is where the bucks are," says Tommy Corn, bagging food to my left, behind this cashier, Donna, who has a great little behind I love to stare at. "And all chicks go for the bucks."

I listen to Tommy, and know he knows.

Everything.

See, Tommy Corn is God's Gift to Women. At least that is what he calls himself. GGTW for short.

Tommy had been in the Navy for about two years before they discharged him. He says it was because his IQ was too high.

Louis and I think it was probably because he looks like Jerry Lewis, and smells like a gorilla.

But we never tell him that.

"When ya got bucks, the chicks dig ya," says Tommy, with his goofy black-framed glasses, messed up hair like he just woke up in the morning, and teeth that went in all directions. Except up.

"Yeah Tabb," says Louis, who's bagging on my right side. "The chicks want bucks and good looks. And you have neither."

Tommy and Louis both have a good laugh.

And I would have too, but I was too infatuated with my cashier Patty, whose brother David had gone to school with me before he went to jail for grand theft auto.

"Ignore them George," says Patty with her beautiful green eyes that look excellent against her green Publix uniform. "I think you're cute, and any girl would consider you a catch."

I blush as I push the current load of groceries into the muggy Tallahassee parking lot, where the dog in the back of the truck actually bites off part of my shirt.

Whatever.

Patty said I was cute.

*

Later that night, after we're done mopping the floors, and scraping up dried gum with rusty razor blades, we steal a six-pack of Grolsch, and sit in the empty parking lot. drinking.

It was only about ninety-three out, a cool evening along the Redneck Riviera.

"Ya gotta learn what chicks like," explains Tommy to Louis and I, as we sit on the hood of my father's orange Datsun 510 station wagon.

"I know what they like," I tell Tommy as I pop off another rubber top from a bottle of Grolsch. "They like guys who are nice and do the right thing."

"Tabb, my man," says Tommy, God's Gift to Women, "ya got it all wrong."

"Yeah, Tabb," adds Louis. "Tommy's right, you don't know jack shit you sorry ass sucker."

"Oh, like you do," I say to Louis, "like you've been with a girl."

Louis suddenly shuts up.
But Tommy doesn't.

"I have," Tommy says. "I've actually gone all the way."

We gasp.

"Like I said," Tommy Corn explains, "I'm God's Gift to Women."

Louis and I just stare at Tommy, not really knowing whether to believe him. But we kind of have to because he is at least four years older than us.

At least. But it could probably be more like ten.

"What's the inside of a woman feel like?" I ask Tommy, finally starting to ask questions about sex after my disaster with Denise.

Tommy just looks at Louis and I, shaking his head.

"You guys really wanna know what the inside of a pussy feels like?" he asks.

We both nod our heads furiously.

The only vaginas we probably ever touched were our mother's when we were born.

"Well," says Tommy, as sweat drips down his face and onto his slimy bottle of Grolsch, "I'll tell ya what, I'm gonna tell ya."

We couldn't wait for this.

God's Gift to Women was going to lay the truth upon us. We were all ears.

And all drunk, too.

"Take your fingers and put them inside your mouths," instructs Tommy Corn.

We eagerly do as we're told.

"Now rub your fingers along the inside of your cheeks," continues Tommy, who looks like he's getting a thrill from this little demonstration.

We do.

I can taste the dried dirt, sweat, and mopping fluid along with the beer on my sweaty fingers.

"Now that," says God's Gift to Women, "is what a pussy feels like. Inside and out!"

Later that night, I go home, open a *Penthouse* magazine I steal from my brother Luke to a pictorial with a blonde girl on a leopard skin rug.

I masturbate with my right hand.

I put my entire left one in my mouth, and make believe it's a vagina.

Unfortunately, my jaw locks open, like it sometimes does when I yawn, and all I can say during dinner that evening is "I cwan't cwose my moue."

*

Everyday after school was the same.

Work.

And the nights were spent drunk or thinking of getting drunk.

And of course, thinking about losing my virginity.

And the closest I'd come to that happened on a Friday or Saturday night, near midnight.

Because that's when *The Rocky Horror Picture Show* would start rolling at the theater on North Monroe Street.

And it was glorious.

Well, should have been, anyway.

*

I first saw *Rocky Horror* at the Waverly Theater in New York City.

I was sixteen. My mom and Nick told me it was a great and funny film, and that I would enjoy it as much as any Mel Brooks or Woody Allen flick. Then they took me.

When I got to the theater, there were all these freaky people in fucked-up makeup crawling all over the place.

And then there was me, with my parents.

When the movie began, people started screaming at the screen, and throwing stuff like rice, toilet paper, and confetti. It was kind of neat.

Then on the screen, to my own personal horror, I saw a guy in women's underwear sing, "I'm just a sweet transvestite, from Transsexual, Transylvania," and that's when I kind of lost it.

I looked, confused, at my mom and Nick, wondering why the hell they had taken me to a movie where men dressed as women and then had sex with other men.

I think I started to believe what my stepmom and dad had been saying about my mom and Nick.

That they did worship Satan, were heroin dealers, and were going to sell me into a white child slavery ring.

Goose bumps popped up all over me.

As the movie continued, I really did begin to get into the music. But I didn't let on. I also really liked seeing all those people around us getting naked.

It was incredible.

Pants, shirts, and underwear were being exchanged freely like we were in a coed locker room. I saw lots of bare breasts, and even some pubic hair. It totally ruled.

Of course, I thought my mom and Nick were complete perverts for taking me to see this, but at the time, it didn't matter. There were naked people surrounding us. Wow!

And it seemed to me the message of the film was "Don't Dream It, Be It," like everyone sang. And truer words to me were never spoken.

So I got addicted.

Hook, line, and fishnets.

*

I saw *Rocky Horror* plenty more times in New York City before moving to Florida.

First, at the Waverly Theater, then at its new home, the 8th Street Playhouse.

A very important location for reasons that will become clear later. But for now, let's just say I was *Rocky Horror* crazy.

I burned through two copies of the motion picture record, and was on my third when I actually arrived in Florida. I also had the Roxy version, the London version and that wacky Australian version on vinyl.

And the more I'd listen to the songs, the more I'd understand them.

Although, written with tongue planted firmly in cheek, this was no ordinary horror movie musical. It was a religion. A cult.

And I was its slave.

*

So every Friday and Saturday at midnight, I would go over to theater on North Monroe and see my favorite movie. And with me would be my *Rocky Horror* friends.

There was Louis, my bag boy buddy with the owl glasses. Then there was Sally, a real college girl who liked to dress as Columbia. And Tammy, who liked to dress as Magenta, and although she could never find a maid's costume big enough to fit her, we always thought she looked swell anyway.

Of course there was Bill, who did Brad. He was another college student who was majoring in drama.

And Marlene, who dressed as Janet, even though she too was oversized, and way too old for the part. But none of that mattered those Friday and Saturday nights. We were dressed up as characters, not ourselves.

We had found a way to escape.

Then there was Ginny, who did Dr. Scott, and finally there was Courtney.

Courtney.

Courtney who did the best Frank-N-Furter south of New York.

I dressed as Riff Raff every once in a while, but mostly I was the Sal Piro of Tallahassee. Sal ran the *Rocky Horror* fan club in New York, doing the shows at the Waverly, and other theaters later on.

He was sort of my unofficial hero, and he even talked to me once.

I couldn't stop telling my mom and Nick and my brothers for days.

Finally they told me to can it.

Anyway, I kind of ran *Rocky Horror* in the city of Tallahassee, in the state of Floriduh.

In fact, I was the one who convinced the theater owners to play it every weekend. I promised them a big following, and lots of money. Which, of course, they eventually got.

*

Every Friday and Saturday, as the lights would dim at midnight and the giant lips would fill up the entire screen, we'd be sitting in the back row waiting to throw stuff, talking back to the characters, and even running up to the front of the theater to act out our scenes.

At first I liked Sally, the college student who played Columbia, the best.

I'd met her at the third or fourth screening of the movie, and she looked really awesome in her sequined skirts and blazer. She wore bright colored make up and had beautiful red hair. She'd always smile at me, and I couldn't help but smile back.

One night, I got up enough courage to talk to her, and found her to be really sweet.

And at least five years older than me.

She's the one who introduced me to Bill, Marlene, Ginny, Tammy, and just about everyone else besides Louis. They too were all in college, or going to grad school, and way older than me.

Upon first meeting them, I lied and told them I too was in college.

But fat mouth Louis told them otherwise, and that's why I think I never really got anywhere with Sally.

Although I did make out with her in her driveway one morning after seeing *Rocky Horror* and a heavy night of drinking.

I remember having my second French kiss, ever, and it tasting like cherries and an ashtray. As we kissed, she also reminded me to breathe, while the Roxy version of *The Rocky Horror Picture Show* blasted on her Honda's stereo. Every once in a while she'd stop to put on more candy flavored lip balm.

"So, you are in high school, huh?" said Sally, as we sat in her car on Nez Perce Drive.

"Yeah," I answered, "but I'm more mature than those children."

"Have you ever taken a lover?" she asked.

I told her that I had taken many lovers, and was a real pro.

She just laughed, and kissed me some more.

She knew.

*

As the weekends passed, I fell more and more in love with Sally.

Even though we never made out after that morning, I still felt a strong place for her in my heart, and figured, maybe, just maybe, she'd see me for the man I wasn't.

But it never really happened, and my fantasy ended when she started seeing this guy who was a hot shot in some local top forty band.

"I just want to be friends," she told me, under those awful fluorescent lights at the local Denny's, where all us freaks would gather after the movie.

"And I just want to die," my brain told me.

And I think my penis agreed.

*

But I just couldn't seem to lose interest in Sally.

One night, she invited Louis and I to a post *Rocky Horror* party at Ginny's pad, and, like the two high school idiots we were, we went.

Drunk.

Before we arrive at Ginny's house, Louis and I drink an entire bottle of Banker's Reserve Rum. The worst and cheapest brand of booze we could find at the ABC Liquor Lounge. We mix it with Coke in giant Burger King cups we get at a drive-through, and the wax actually melts off the sides of the cup.

As we finish off the bottle in the Publix parking lot, listening to Dead Boys on my dad's car stereo, my cup collapses completely from the rum and spills all over me.

But I don't care.

I'm so wasted I can hardly see.

Which, means, of course, it was time to drive to the party.

I somehow navigate the car down Tennessee Street, trying to stay between the flashing white lines that keep disappearing. I think I'm doing a great job until a cop pulls us over.

At first I'm confused about the flashing lights. I haven't smoked pot again.

Then I remember where I am and what I should never have been doing.

"Driver's license and registration," says the cop in his blue and white helmet and sunglasses, as I roll down my window.

"My what?" I yell, over the Dead Boys' "Ain't Nothing to Do."

"Sir, turn down the stereo and give me your driver's license and registration," yells the cop, with stinky fish breath.

And I hate fish.

I give the shark my stuff, turn down the stereo, and look at Louis.

"I told you I should have been driving," says Louis. "You're drunk!"

For some reason, the cop says nothing, just starts writing something down.

So we sit there, in my father's Datsun 510 station wagon, parked on the side of Tennessee Street, with a cop car next to us, flashing lights and all. They start to make me dizzy and I hope like hell I don't puke.

Finally the cop opens his stinky fish mouth. I'm convinced he's going to give me that drunk driver test, and from there it will straight to a Florida jail, where'd they'll tell me to "Squeal like a pig, Jew boy!"

"Sir," says Officer Tuna Breath, "are you aware you have a right tail light out?"

I don't say anything.

I'm in shock.

"I am issuing you a ticket," he continues. "If you have it fixed within a week, you don't have to pay the fine."

And with that he gives me the piece of paper he's written on, and then he's off into the Tallahassee night.

I just look at Louis, and he looks at me. I crank up the Dead Boys, and we make our way toward the party.

*

As we pull into Ginny's driveway, I remember "bumping" into the rear fender of Sally's Honda Civic. I figure she won't notice the dent on it.

Until she picks it up off the ground.

Inside the house, Louis and I find Heaven. Four college girls, and a bathtub filled with grain alcohol and Hawaiian Punch.

"Listen George," says Sally, in a sort of firm voice. "Grain alcohol is very strong stuff, it can make you extremely drunk."

I tell Sally that I drink it all the time and that I'm a pro.

She gives me that all knowing look, again.

Four or five huge plastic cups of grain and punch later, I find myself making out with Sally on Ginny's couch. The Ramones tape I brought over is blaring, and every few minutes I stop kissing her, stand up, and scream, "Hey Ho, Let's Go!"

Then Sally and I would continue to make out like crazy, and I soon find myself touching her breasts.

A breakthrough.

As I'm kissing her nipples over her shirt, I see Louis staring over at me.

In shock.

"What are you looking at, ya sorry ass sucker?" I yell at Louis using his own words.

He says nothing and just smiles as he drinks another cup of grain and punch.

I then look over to the other side of the room and see Ginny, Tammy, and Sally watching us go at it.

"Cool," I think.

I return my attention to Sally's nipples. They're like Heaven on Earth.

I continue to kiss and make out with Sally, and somehow in the depths of my mind, wonder where the cherry and ash tray taste went.

But it didn't matter. I was getting all hot and sweaty with Sally, and soon she'd ask me to take her on as her lover.

"Hey Ho, Let's Go!" I yell once again, taking a brief break. Then I fall back on Sally and have a look around the room.

Louis is still smiling, which is starting to piss me off, as are Ginny, Tammy, and Sally.

I start doing that tongue dance again, then stop.

Ginny, Tammy, and Sally?

What the fuck?

My heart starts to beat real fast and I quickly come to the conclusion that I'm dead again. That I'm seeing this whole thing from the great beyond, and I really did never come back that awful day after I smoked that joint.

Then I try and get a grip on reality.

I look down at Sally again, and this time, try really hard to focus my eyes. She looks fuzzy, and is almost topless.

I look again.

And again.

And once more, with all the strength my drunken eyes can muster, I see Marlene beneath me.

And then I do what any other healthy American red-blooded male would do.

I pass out.

*

I wake up the next morning next to Louis on the floor of Ginny's house. As he rubs the sleep from his eyes he tells me that I did great with Marlene a few hours earlier.

So I throw up on him.

Somehow we make it out to my car, and I start to drive us both home. As I drive, I imagine I'm flying an airplane, and Louis is my copilot.

"Tallahassee," I say into my CB radio, "this is Anarchy Air number six-six-sixer, are we cleared for take off?"

Louis laughs and tells me to concentrate on the road.

When I ask him "What road?" he takes over control of the aircraft and somehow manages to get us home to my mansion on the plantation.

As Louis and I stagger into my father's white dream at eight in the morning, stinking of booze and puke, we see my dad at the kitchen table.

"Hiya pop," I say to my dad, fishnet stockings worn over my jeans for some reason.

"Um, hello Mr. Tabb," adds Louis.

"How did you get home?" my dad yells at both of us.

"Louis flew the plane, Dad, I went in the back with the stewardesses," I slur, drunkenly.

I see Louis fight to hold back a smile.

"George, go to your fucking room," yells my dad, "and I'll call Louis's parents. You are grounded. Forever."

"So that's how long?" I spit out.

It was then my dad grabbed me by the back of my jeans and dragged me to my room.

I spent the next three days trying to stop throwing up blood.

*

One night about a week later, Bill, who likes dressing as Brad Majors, and I are hanging out in my dad's car in the movie theater parking lot, getting drunk.

"George," he says to me, "you're really cool, ya know? And you look hot!"

I look at Bill.

"Um," I stammer, "you look really hot in your corset, fishnets, pumps and girlie underwear." I add, "And I think you're cool, too."

"You really think so?" Bill asks.

"Yeah," I lie.

"Do you like me George?" asks Bill in a low voice, one I've never heard him use before.

I tell him I do, and that he's very nice and all.

"I mean, do you *like* me?" he asks again.

Again I tell him I think he's a very pleasant fellow and fun to be around, even though he drinks way too much Wild Turkey.

"I mean," says Bill, "do you think I'm cute?"

"Um, sure," I say, confused.

"Have you ever taken a man as your lover?" he then asks.

I look at him, and finally understand where the conversation is going.

"Uh, um, no," I say, then try to make him feel better, "but I haven't taken a woman as one either."

"Well, George," he says as he looks me in the eyes from behind his black framed Brad Majors glasses with no lenses, "I think you and I should make love."

I don't say anything.

I don't know what to say.

He's my pal and all, and I don't want to hurt his feelings, and he does have rather hot legs.

"Wouldn't it be nice?" Bill asks in a very Frank-N-Furter voice.

I think about it for a few more seconds, and suddenly Bill is right in my face, with his tongue down my throat.

"Bill," I said to him as I gently push him away. "I don't think I'm ready for this."

"You don't like me? You don't like the way I dress?" he cries out, hurt.

I looked at his fishnets and girlie underwear, and had to admit that it did give me a boner, but, alas, that just wasn't enough.

"You look beautiful Bill, just like Brad," I try to explain, "but I'm not ready for that, yet. Maybe some other time?"

"Fuck you, George," he yells.

Then Bill opens the car door, and storms out in his fishnets and black pumps.

"I'm sorry," I yell to him as he stomps across the parking lot.

He just flips me off.

As I watch him walk away, I have to admit to myself that he does have a nice ass.

*

Two weekends and many drinks later, I find myself in my father's car with Courtney before the movie.

In the same parking spot.

"You make a great Frank-N-Furter," I say to her as she sits there, in her black cape, black lipstick, black makeup, black fishnets, black wig.

"You're too kind," is her reply, in a voice as low and sexy as Tim Curry's.

We sit in my car listening to the London version of *The Rocky Horror Picture Show*, noticing the differences in Tim's vocal texture.

"He's so sexy," Courtney says as she closes her eyes and sings along.

"So are you," I say back to her.

She opens her eyes, and I see these beautiful blue orbs staring into my soul.

"You think I'm pretty?" she asks, out of character for a few seconds.

I tell her I think she's great.

Without her wardrobe she has beautiful blondish red hair, and a wonderful smile. With her wardrobe, she is the hottest, well, thing, ever.

"Thank you, George," she says, then leans over and kisses me. Tongue and all.

The next thing I know I'm sitting in my car making out with Dr. Frank-N-Furter.

We are kissing and touching and I get really, really excited. In between kisses, she falls in and out of character, saying things like "Isn't this nice," and "In just seven days, I can make you a man."

Finally I get up enough courage and put my hands on her breasts.

But I couldn't feel them.

"Um," I stammer.

"They're taped down, I have to be the best Frank, you know," whispers Courtney in my ear.

So I feel up her taped down breasts.

And it's kind of nice.

We keep kissing and I feel Courtney's gloved hand slide under my shirt and up my chest, and it feels swell to the point of tears.

And that is when I go for it.

I drop my hand to her crotch.

I start to feel around her leather underwear, on the outside, and find a huge bulge.

I stop.

"What's wrong?" whispers Dr. Frank-N-Furter in my ear, "don't you like it?"

I don't know what to say.

"You mean to tell me you don't like being with a man?" she whispers in character in my ear, and then slides her hand inside my pants and actually gives my testicles a hard squeeze.

I let out a small yelp, and then kiss her more as I think about my situation.

I wouldn't make out with Bill, who was a man dressed as a man dressed as a woman. But I am making out with a woman dressed as a man dressed as a woman.

It all starts making me dizzy.

"I, um," I stammer, then trying to say the right thing, "I've never been with a man before."

Suddenly Courtney stops kissing me, and lets go of my penis, which she's actually wrapped her hand around.

"How could you say that?" she yells at me. "I'm a woman."

"I know?" I say, really confused.

"Fuck you, George," she says, then opens the car door, and climbs out in her fishnets and black pumps.

"I'm sorry," I yell to her as she stomps away.

She just flips me off.

As I watch her walk away, I have to admit to myself that she does have a nice ass.

*

The following weeks fly by as Louis and I continue to bag groceries and listen to the wisdom of Tommy Corn, God's Gift to Women.

When I tell Tommy that I actually touched more than one pair of breasts, he steals me a whole case of Grolsch after closing, which we drink while pissing into the coleslaw in the deli department.

"Tabb," he says, as he whizzes into the metallic bin, "touching titty is great, but soon you'll be eating pussy."

I quickly wonder why anyone would want to eat a cat, but then forget about it as I watch Tommy switch from the coleslaw to the pickles.

A few days later, while bagging, Patty, my favorite cashier, asks me to come to the back to help her count her register.

I do.

When we get into the back office with the cement covered walls, Patty grabs me by my clip-on tie and pushes her tongue through my teeth and, like Bill, down my throat.

"What's that for?" I ask after she stops the boxing match in our mouths.

"For you," she replies, and then, as quickly as she made her way to the back of the store, she returns to the front.

When I return a few minutes later, after spending some quality time with myself on a toilet seat in the men's room, Tommy and Louis just glare at me.

"George," I hear Henry slur behind me, "may I have a word with you?"

I say "Sure" and he walks me off to the side of the store.

"You have lipstick all over your face," Henry says. Then he gives me a cloth handkerchief to wipe it off.

I thank him, clean my face in the bakery department's glass case reflection, and start to make my way back to the front.

"She likes you," Henry whispers. "They all like you."

I look at Henry, and for the first time don't see the horseshoe mark on his forehead. "Don't listen to a word of that bullshit Tommy and Louis tell you," Henry continues, "keep up the good work, and by this time next year, you'll have girls all over you like flies on shit. By then I might even make you stock boy."

I thank Henry and start my way back to the front, for some reason returning all the fallen cans and boxes to their rightful places.

*

Very soon after that comes *Rocky Horror*'s six month anniversary in Tallahassee, Floriduh.

The night of the show we all go to Ginny's house and get into our costumes. Bill lends me the gold lamé outfit he likes to wear to local discos, and Sally lends me a blond wig she says drives her boyfriend wild.

I find a banana in Ginny's refrigerator, and Marlene weaves it into Sally's wig.

I look in the mirror after they put make up on me and I look just like Riff Raff in that final scene where he kills the good doctor and his boy toy.

Sally wears her sequined outfit, and Tammy, her under-sized French maid costume. Bill looks wonderful in the new fishnets and pumps he brags about buying at the mall that day, and Courtney is absolutely stunning.

Tommy Corn and Louis are with us as well, running final errands, and helping the women put on or take off their clothes.

And each can't stop smiling.

We then make our way to North Monroe Street.

At exactly midnight, the theater's lights dim, and the lips come up on the screen. We all shout and squeal with delight, and sing along to every word.

Then, when the action starts on screen, we go up front and do our first complete floor show. One that would make Sal Piro proud.

As the night continues, I feel a real sense of family with this strange group of people. With Bill, a guy who wants to be a girl, and Courtney, a girl who wants to be a guy.

With Tammy and Sally, both great friends who I knew I'd never forget.

With Marlene and Ginny, who gave me great mammories.

And Louis and Tommy, guys who helped me define the word "friendship."

*

After the song "Rose Tint My World," an important dance number in the movie, it's time for my big appearance. I come out singing "Frank-N-Furter, it's all over," while Louis and Tommy shine flashlights upon Tammy and me. I sing the words loud and proud.

I know my dad is somewhere in the audience, and although I know he hates all my friends and calls them "fags," I know he must be proud of me somewhere in his heart. Why else would he be there?

I finish my part, and then while watching Courtney sing an emotionally charged version of "I'm Going Home," I start to weep.

As I listen to her voice, along with Tim Curry's, I know that's the song I want played at my funeral.

It's a song that says it all.

I look over at Sally and Tammy as Courtney finishes the song, and they are in tears as well. As are Ginny, Marlene, Bill, and even Louis and Tommy Corn.

We are sharing an important time in our lives, and somehow, we know it.

The air has become magic, and when we all go up in front of the screen as the movie ends, we hold each other's hands during our standing ovation.

*

Many years later I found out my father was a closet transvestite.

And to this day, I really wish he had told me.

It was the one thing I could have understood about the man, and perhaps, just perhaps, it could have made us closer.

We could have shared fishnets, underwear, and maybe a little of our souls.

A DEAL'S A DEAL

SO THERE I AM, wearing my stupid clip-on tie, late for work at Publix. My jeans are riding up my crotch, and I can feel the ridges in the car's gas pedal against my socks through my holey Woolworth Converse high-top knock offs.

Soon I hope I'll have enough money saved to buy some real sneakers. Along with some new clothes. Everything seems two sizes too small for me, but my father and stepmother refuse to spend one dime on me.

In fact, I'm driving to work in their orange Datsun 510 station wagon, with a tank full of gas I should have paid for. Of course, my sister, Diana, gets to use the car without paying for the gas, as does Cybill. My father tells me it's his car, and if I want use it, I pay.

Which sort of makes sense. In his twisted way.

Anyway, I'm breaking the speed limit because I know if I get to work late, Tommy Corn and Louis are going to work behind the good cashiers, and I'll get stuck with Cindy Lang, this awful woman in her mid-forties who, behind everyone's back, says some really nasty shit.

And she always smells like raw fish. Fuck that.

So, I'm hauling ass on route 319 and suddenly, off to my right, I see Her.

She's wearing a pair of Daisy Duke cutoff blue jeans that are riding up her crotch and a neon tube top that shows off her quarter-sized nipples, and she's licking a vanilla ice cream cone. Slowly.

Feeling my penis begin to swell, I totally forget I'm behind the wheel of a fast moving motor vehicle. After I pass this natural wonder, I look back at her in my rearview mirror.

Her shorts are literally displaying both cheeks of her fine and young, firm butt, and the dripping vanilla ice cream all over the back of her arms nearly makes me orgasm.

As "Touch-a, Touch-a, Touch-a Me" from *The Rocky Horror Picture Show* blares on the car's stereo, my mind leaps to warp nine and suddenly I'm in bed with this beautiful creature.

Of course, this meant I couldn't see the row of cars parked at the red light in the middle of the street, only fifty feet in front of me.

It was weird, but at that point, the only grounding I had to reality was the feeling of my hard penis rubbing against the steering wheel.

But let me back up a bit.

*

When I first got my driver's license at sixteen in Greenwich, Connecticut, my father immediately grounded me for a year. And in that year, he let me drive his cars twice. Once, on an errand in which I broke his Suburban's A-Frame, then, to Florida, where he moved us to Water Oak Plantation. His kingdom.

While not happy about always having to ride my bicycle everywhere, like the eight miles to high school, I soon learned, like my brother Luke, to hitchhike.

Every conversation in every car was the same.

"Do your parents know you are doing this?" they'd ask, in wonder.

I'd explain to them I was an orphan, like Luke told me to say, and that I was on the way to live with an aunt or uncle.

This would usually result in a kind smile, and sometimes, a few extra bucks for our pockets.

We really did depend on the kindness of strangers.

Anyway, once I got the job bagging groceries after school at Publix, full time, the question became whether George got to drive one of his father's ten automotive vehicles or had to be picked up at work every night around midnight.

Cybill made the right decision by telling my father, "If you're up at that fucking hour, you pick the little shit up. Me? No fucking way. He's your little bastard."

So my dad, for once in his life, did the nice thing and let me use his Datsun 510 station wagon to go to and from work.

As long as I promised to keep the gas tank filled.

Which I did.

But not with my gas.

His.

You see, he'd installed this gas pump thing near one of our garages, well, *behind* one of our garages.

Every month a gas truck would show up and fill the large underground tank hidden beneath the plantation.

And it would stink.

And every time the guy would fill the tank, he'd tell my father that we sure went through a lot of gasoline.

My dad would nod his head, and say it takes a lot of fuel to run the world of Lester Tabb.

What he didn't know was that it took a lot of fuel to run the car his son drove, as well as about ten other vehicles owned by his two sons' friends.

See, Luke and I, one night while snooping around my father's office, found a Yale key taped to the bottom of his pipe collection display.

Immediately knowing what it must have been for, Luke filled the Dune Buggy he recently purchased, and I then filled the Datsun.

The next night after my parents were asleep, I called around five friends, as did Luke. We played gas station attendant all night, and suddenly, we were everyone's best pals.

Every time we were finished, we'd just tape the key back where we found it, and we were never caught.

Ever.

Those were the days.

*

Anyway, I'm late for work and going about fifty in a thirty mile an hour zone when I plow into the row of cars stopped at the red light at Timberlane Mall and Route 319.

The whole thing happens like in those movies where everything turns into slow motion. I find myself slamming on the Datsun 510's already worn down brakes and hear a loud grinding noise that sounds awful.

Then I start to smell smoke, see sparks, and the next thing I know, I'm parked in the rear end of some pickup truck.

Things suddenly go back into real time, and I run out of my father's car to see the damage done to this poor person's pickup. The guy who owns the truck hops out of the cab, and he looks very Hispanic, what with his thick black mustache and all.

"Holy Jesus," he sighs. "Weren't jew watching where jew were going?" he asks.

I'm in too much shock to say anything, and besides, I'm crying.

"Cheer up little man," says the mustache. "Look, no damage to my truck, eh?"

I look at the back of his vehicle, and to my surprise, he's right. There's just a tiny scratch on his fender.

"Looks like jew got the problem," says the guy as he gets closer to me, looking at my father's totaled car.

I look at it with him and see that the entire front end of the Datsun 510 station wagon has shrunk quite a few feet. It looks like an orange accordion, and I feel more tears run down my face.

Finally, I speak.

"Should I call the police?" I sob.

"Are jew fucking nuts?" the man says five inches from my face.

He reeks of alcohol.

"I don't even have a license, eh? It's best jew just drive off and we make believe this never happened, *comprende, amigo?*"

I just nod as I watch him get in his truck and speed off into the sunny Tallahassee afternoon.

*

Somehow, the car is still able to move really slowly when I push on the gas pedal.

I decide it would be best to drive the thing the three and a half miles back to Water Oak, where I'm sure my dad will castrate me, then hang me from one of his beautiful trees on those rounded grassy green hills.

But he doesn't do either.

To my surprise, he takes a look at the car and is scarily calm.

"George," he says in a tone I never knew he possessed, "had a bad day, huh?"

I tell my father I did, then begin to slowly sob.

Finally, he understood. Or remembered what it was like to be a kid my age.

"So you trashed my car, big deal," he says, and with that, puts his arms around me.

I hug him tight and smile in a weird way I hadn't done in years.

"Well," my father says calmly, as he gently pushes me away, "it seems to me you have two options."

"Okay," I sob with joy.

My father loves me. He really does.

"One," he says, "is to take it to Sheffield's Auto-Body repair shop and have it fixed."

Then he's silent.

"The other?" I ask.

"Two," he continues, "you can buy that wrecked bucket of bolts from me for the Blue Book value."

Knowing I've got only five hundred bucks saved up in the bank, plus two hundred in cash buried in a coffee can near the barn, I know I'm fucked.

"What do you say?" my father asks calmly.

"I don't think I have enough money for either," I try to calmly tell him.

Suddenly, Cybill bursts through the kitchen door, passing the bruised and battered Datsun 510 orange station wagon on her way up the outside steps.

"What the fuck happened," she yells, as she sees me with my father in the kitchen.

"George had a little accident," my dad tells my stepmother, "and we're taking care of it like adults."

"Adults?" Cybill screams. "That little turd just destroyed your car and you are taking care of it 'like adults?'"

"Yes," my father says calmly.

"Well then you're just as much of a pussy as your idiot sons," yells my stepbitch. "Why don't you just buy George his own god damn car? A Mercedes, like you always promised me!"

"Listen woman," seethes my father, "don't take that tone with me."

"What tone?" she shrieks. "The one that says you're a nothing of a father, never mind a poor provider plus an impotent piece of shit?"

"Fuck you," my father yells at Cybill.

Then all hell breaks loose.

Cybill grabs a steak knife from the kitchen counter and runs with it at my father.

He deflects the blade's point, and it goes into my upper shoulder.

A small flesh wound.

They continue fight, hand to hand, with Cybill yanking out Lester's hair, and Lester landing really heavy left and right hooks to her fat ugly face.

"Go Dad," I almost find myself saying, but know it's best to keep my mouth shut.

They continue to fight, and when it's over, Cybill's face is bloody and swollen, and my dad's curly brown hair is in clumps on the kitchen floor.

I look at them both and just want to die.

Finally, my father speaks.

"George, you little fuck," he says to me, more like himself, "you either get that fucking car fixed or you buy it from me. Now."

I try and tell him I have no money, and I see Cybill laugh as tiny drips of blood seep from the sides of her mouth.

"Look you little good-for-nothing," my dad yells, "you and THAT car leave my property immediately, and don't return until either it's fixed, or you've purchased it."

I try to think of something to say but can't.

So, with my head hung low, and clip-on tie hanging off my collar, I make my way outside to my father's rusted out and now destroyed Datsun 510 station wagon.

I try and feel sorry, sad, or guilty.

But all I can feel is rage.

As I start the broken car, and begin to back it away from my father's rebuild of Tara from *Gone With the Wind*, in the kitchen window I see Cybill and my father begin going at it again.

I hope one of them kills the other as I drive slowly away from home.

*

With nowhere else to go, I grind the station wagon toward my friend Scott's house. He lives with his mom in a sort of apartment/condo complex, complete with pool and lakeside view.

As the car screeches to a halt in front of my pal's place, Scott's mom comes out in her underwear, as usual, with rollers in her hair.

As long as I'd known Scott and had gone to his house after school or on weekends, his mom had walked around half naked, and no one ever gave her a second glance. At first, it seemed strange to me, but soon it became almost invisible.

Like my pubic hair.

Anyway, Scott's mother rubs her chin as she stares at the orange accordion. She looks me in the eyes, then at my clip-on tie.

My clip-on tie!

Fuck!

I'd forgot to call Publix and tell them what happened. So I ask Scott's mom to use the phone, and I get Henry, my floor manager, on the line.

"Where are you, George?" slurs Henry, a bit agitated.

I tell him the truth.

"I'm sick at home with a hundred and seven degree fever," I say, sounding as ill as possible.

He tells me I should stay home, drink plenty of fluids, and have my parents take care of me. I sort of wince at the last part, then thank him for understanding.

Five minutes later, Scott walks in his front door as I'm telling his mom, who's sitting in her underwear on a couch next to me, chain smoking, about my little accident.

I explain my situation to Scott as well.

"So," says Scott, with his balding blonde hair and wire rim glasses, plus a new mustache he'd just grown to go with the hairy blonde chest he was so proud of showing off, "you either fix it, buy it, or run away".

I tell him the run away thing sounds the best, and it's probably my only option.

Scott tells me he knows lots about cars, and has learned tons of cool things from his older brother, Bill, who was a movie projectionist over at Florida State University.

"Tell you what," says Scott, as he gently pats me on the shoulder, "let's take the car over to Sheffield's Auto and see what they have to say."

We do.

They tell us it'll cost at least one thousand dollars to fix the front end. The front panels are trashed, the hood, scrap metal, and they're surprised the car even runs at all.

We thank them and then return to Scott's mom at her house. In her underwear.

"I'm so fucking dead," I moan to Scott, feeling my world come to an end.

"Didn't your dad mention Blue Book value?" Scott asks.

I tell him he did, but I have no clue what that is.

Scott runs to his room, and returns with a Blue Book.

Doh.

It's got all the values of current and past cars, and what they sell for, used.

We find the Datsun 510 station wagon and the best price for one at the time is seven hundred bucks.

Exactly as much money as I could get my hands on that day.

Scott tells me to call my dad and tell him we're coming over with the money to buy the car.

When I ask him why I should even buy a car that won't go over ten miles an hour, he just gives me that know-it-all Scott smile, and says, "Call your dad!"

So I call my father and arrange to meet him at a Burger King between Water Oak Plantation and Scott's house. There is no way the crushed car will make it any further.

My dad shows up twenty minutes late, and I give him seven hundred dollars in cash. I've emptied my bank account, and Scott's mom gave us the rest from the money she had hidden under her mattress.

She knew I was good for it.

And I was. I repaid her the next day.

Anyway, as we sit in Burger King, me, unable to look my father in the eyes, Scott shows him the Blue Book, and that seven hundred dollars is the most he could ever hope for with that make, model, and year of that car.

My father, thinking he's made an excellent sale, smiles widely. He and Scott shake hands, and I remain invisible.

Which is fine.

The deal is done.

We then return to Scott's house again, where something magical happens.

*

When we pull into Scott's driveway, peering furiously over the crushed hood, we see Bill, Scott's older brother. Scott has told me in the past that he is excellent with cars, and almost knew about more things them he did.

Almost.

Also greeting us is Scott's mom.

In her underwear, this time leopard print.

"Looks like you fucked up that rusted out pile of bolts," says Bill, who looks almost identical to Scott, mustache and all. The only difference is Bill's hair is darker. Like his mom's.

"That rusted pile of bolts I now own," I explain, looking at the thing, figuring I could get about twenty-five bucks in parts for it.

"Cool," says Bill. "Mom told me you were buying it. That's why I'm here!"

"Huh?" I say, confused.

"Scott, go in the house and get that huge chain dad left behind when he disappeared into that bottle all those years ago," says Bill. "Mom, George and I are gonna move this thing over next to that tree."

Bill points at a huge oak tree on the other side of the parking lot and I wonder what the fuck he's thinking. I bet he wants me to drive it as fast as it will go into the huge wooden monster, just to finish it off and put it out of its suffering.

Scott returns with a chain that's probably as heavy as any of us, and Bill has me park directly in front of the huge oak.

What happens next is straight out of The A-Team. And as it's being done, I can't help thinking about my father.

Finally, I say "I pity the fool" out loud.

"Who?" asks Scott. "Your dad, Mr. T?""

I nod my head.

Scott and Bill have wrapped the heavy chain around the front end of the car, over the radiator, but in front of the motor. The rest of the chain is around the huge oak tree.

They've also torn off the hood from the car and put it over next to another tree close by.

"We want you to get back in *your* car," explains Bill, "and back it up. Slowly."

I do as I'm told.

At first the car moves kind of quickly, but when the chain begins to tighten, the car stops moving.

"Okay, now," says Bill while Scott nods his head, "when I tell you to, floor it!"

I get ready to do as I'm told as Scott and his brother each take their places in front of my car and start to push.

"Now!" yells Bill, and I give the car all it's got.

At first the wheels just spin and it doesn't go anywhere.

Then, slowly, the thing starts to move backwards, a few inches every ten seconds, as we hear the sound of metal screeching and scraping.

This goes on for about a minute and finally Scott gives me the "kill it" motion by running his right index finger over his neck.

I turn off the car and get out.

As I do, I see Scott and Bill high-fiving one another.

The car is stretched back out to its normal size.

Holy fuck!

An hour later, with the help of their mom and a few rubber mallets, we've managed to bend the hood back into it's proper shape. Sure it has a few dents, but when Bill bolts it down to the front of the Datsun 510, it closes perfectly.

"Do you mind if I try and give it a spin?" asks Bill, as Scott and I drag the heavy chain back into his house.

I tell him if he can drive that thing and it works, I'll kiss his feet.

Twenty minutes later, upon returning to his mother's house, he takes his socks off and I kiss every single toe.

"Guess what?" says Bill, as he puts his sneakers and socks back on.

"What?" asks Scott.

"That's what!" says Bill.

They both laugh.

And I find myself doing the same. Although it's the stupidest joke in the world, that day, it was the coolest thing I'd ever heard.

Anyway, Bill walks over to a bag he just got from a hardware store, and tells me he's brought me a present.

For being such a good pal to his younger brother.

He takes out a can of blue spray paint, and a huge piece of cardboard.

"What's that for?" I ask, wondering if maybe he wants to paint my car blue, which was fine by me.

"Just watch, George," says Bill. "You're gonna love this!"

He and Scott take the cardboard out to the drive way along with a couple of Exacto knives. First they draw the

Batman logo with a magic marker on the cardboard, then cut the shape out.

Cool.

I have a cardboard Batman logo. I can put it on the side of the car.

Then Scott and Bill tape down the cardboard to the hood of my car with tons of duct tape we'd found while returning the chain to the basement.

After that, they tape newspaper to the entire front end of the car, and even on the windshield.

Now, all that can be seen of the front of the Datsun 510 station wagon is an orange bat.

I look at both brothers and still don't know where this is going, but I don't really care. To me, they could do no wrong.

Bill and Scott fight over the can of blue spray paint, and, finally, it's decided that they'll take turns.

Bill sprays over the cardboard and fills up the entire bat, then Scott does the same thing twenty minutes later. He says it's the second coat.

Whatever.

As we sit in warm Tallahassee, waiting for paint to dry, I realize this is how exciting the South really is.

The boy's mother brings us all bottles of Michelob, a shit beer if there ever was one, and we guzzle them down, enjoying the rancid after taste.

Then the mother asks if she can do the honors and we all say sure.

She rips off all the duct tape, newspaper, and cardboard, and when I finally see my car again I almost faint.

It's the coolest fucking thing I've ever seen.

An orange Datsun 510 station wagon with a huge Batman bat in neon blue covering its hood.

Tears of joy start rolling down my face.

"Don't cry yet," says Bill, "we've only just begun."

I call my father and tell him I'm spending the night at Scott's, and I'll see him tomorrow, after school.

He tells me he's sorry he's made such a good business decision, but that's the way things went.

I tell him "whatever", hang up the phone, then have some more fun with my new best friends.

*

The next day, after school, I began the long drive home. As I pulled out of the Leon High School parking lot, I cranked up the tape of Jan and Dean's "Batman Theme" on the eight track car stereo Bill told me he just had laying around.

He told me the huge stereo speakers we set up in the back of the beast were just laying around as well. Also the power-ful tiny ones he wired in the front of the car, beneath that Batman covered hood, against the front railing of the car. So everyone could hear me coming.

Or going, as was the case.

Seated next to me was Scott, who was singing along with the "La-la-la-la-la-la-la-la" part of the tune. Covering the entire back of the car with the back seats down, was green shag carpet we'd found in a dumpster behind Payless Carpet during third period.

We skipped almost the rest of the school day and cut the raggedy pieces into the right shapes to fill up the entire orange Batmobile. Then we glued it down with epoxy we stole from the wood shop studio.

And for the *coup de grace*, Bill gave me a pair of black fuzzy dice with the Playboy bunny logo on them.

As well as a cool *Rocky Horror Picture Show* decal, that he somehow put perfectly on to the rear window.

We were stylin'.

And the looks we got from all the other kids at school that day just confirmed what we already knew.

We *were* cool.

*

As we drove up the huge mountains of rolling green hills along Route 319 to Water Oak Plantation, just ten miles from the southern Georgia border, lots of drivers honked at us and gave us the "thumbs-up" signal. Others just laughed or scowled.

But *everyone* had a reaction.

Upon reaching the mansion, Scott and I prepared for what my father might say.

Scott said my dad would just be happy for me.

I told him my dad would probably want his car back.

And, as usual, I was right.

As we parked the Orange Batmobile in front of Water Oak Plantation's mansion, my stepmother as well as my father came out of the house scratching their heads.

Luke and Sam came out as well, and seeing the kick ass Batman logo and shiny wax job we'd given the thing, they smiled, before screaming they both wanted to ride in it.

But we couldn't really hear them. We had the Dead Boys' "Sonic Reducer" cued up to the beginning, where Stiv Bators sings, "Don't need no mom and dad."

After we shut off the car, my father walks around his ex-station wagon, then looks at the both of us.

"Who did this for you?" demands my father.

We tell him we did it ourselves.

"Bullshit," says Cybill. "Your mother and Nick wired you money, didn't they?"

"I'll kill those junkie fucks," seethes Lester as his face turns purple and he begins to shake with rage.

I try to explain that Scott and I, along with Scott's older brother Bill, did the whole thing ourselves, and it really did-n't cost us any money at all.

"Good," says my father, as he digs around his pocket, and pulls out a huge wad of bills, "here's your money back, I'm retaking possession of the car."

I refuse to take his money and tell him a deal's a deal. Like he's always told me.

"The little shit is right," says Cybill. "You say that all the time. If you take back his car, you better give me that Mercedes I wouldn't blow you for!"

Scott laughs under his funny little mustache, but I'm just pissed.

"Your mother's right," my father finally says. "A deal is a deal. You can keep the car."

With that he sticks out his hand out for me to shake.

Surprised at his strange and sudden sense of fairness, I reach out my hand to meet his.

He squeezes so hard I have to ice it down for two days straight.

MY LEATHER JACKET
AND ME

SO, THERE I AM, on a freezing New York City night with my pal, Louis, each of us in our Ramones style leather motorcycle jackets.

Only mine costs well over three hundred bucks, while my bag boy buddy's costs next to zilch. It's one of those fake "pleather" jackets, which looked almost as cool as the real thing, but could only be found at places like Kmart or other discount stores.

It's the winter of my senior year in high school and Louis and I, now total punk rock Ramones fans, are making our way out of New York City's rock club, the Ritz.

We'd just seen some lame band called Huey Lewis and the News for two bucks at the Ritz's Rock 'n' Roll Against Depression night and were in pretty good spirits considering no girls took us up on our offers to dance.

It's really fucking cold as we begin to make our way back to my mom's place on West Fourth Street, and under our motorcycle jackets, real and fake, we're just wearing thin t-shirts. Me, a Sid Vicious one Nick had purchased for me at a local punk boutique called Trash And Vaudeville, and

Louis, a Ramones *Rocket to Russia* shirt, complete with the little picture of the pinhead guy sitting on a missile.

It was the only shirt Louis ever wore. Ever.

As we hunch our shoulders to warm up from the subzero temperatures, I think about what my mom had said before we left the apartment for the evening.

"George," she had said in that motherly way, "I know you guys want to look cool and all, but why don't you wear something warmer?"

Of course, I just pouted at her like a two-year-old.

"No," I said. "You can't make me!"

"You're right," she continued. "I can't make you do anything, but please try and not get sick. You boys want to have fun during your Christmas vacation, don't you?"

I tell her we do, and while I appreciate the idea, now that I'm a Ramone and all, it's just not cool.

She tells me she understands.

As does Nick.

"Mrs. Tabb," Louis then said, even though her last name hadn't been Tabb for many years, "I've tried with your sorry ass sucker of a son to make him wear his winter coat, but he just won't. I'm sorry to have failed you."

I just looked at Louis and seethed. The little fuck, not two minutes earlier, had told me we *had* to wear our leather jackets to the Ritz that night, because it would make us cool, and chicks dug cool guys.

I reminded Louis that his jacket wasn't real leather, and that's when he fed that line of horseshit to my mom.

Bastard.

Anyway, as we're trudging through at least six inches of snow, with more falling upon us on East Tenth Street near Fourth Avenue, two guys approach us.

We can't really make out their faces through the snow, but one guy yells "Yo," so we yell "Yo!" back.

When they approach us we can see they've got the good sense to be wearing those snorkel type jackets, with the big hoods and all.

They're warm.

We're freezing.

"Hey man," says one of the guys as he flips back his hood and lets wet snow gather on his almost shaved head, "You got a light?" The other guy takes off his hood and his hair is short as well.

"Well?" asks the one guy who's talking, "how about it?"

I look at Louis and he looks at me.

"Tabb," he says, "you sorry ass sucker, get out your lighter for the gentlemen."

I look at him pissed. I'm tired of that term, and my hands are so fucking cold in my blue-jean pockets, I'm afraid to take them out and use them. They'd probably get frostbite and fall off, then I'd never be able to play with myself again. I'd have to depend on girls for that, which, I knew, was never going to happen.

So I take out my frozen right hand, unzip the front right pocket on my shiny new leather jacket with the Ramones-style Air Force U.S. pins, and all Nick and I had found at an army navy store. I grasp the black lighter with the Playboy logo on it I'd found at a cool ass head shop a couple of days earlier, and start to remove it.

The next thing I know I'm laying on the hood of a snow-covered car with the sweet tasting flavor of blood in my mouth, and my nose hurts so bad I feel my eyes swelling.

"Give us your leather jackets!" says the guy who hadn't spoken before.

"Fuck you," I spit blood at them.

"Give us your leather jackets and we won't hurt you anymore," says the first guy, as he hits me in the gut with a lead pipe he's pulled out of nowhere.

"No fucking way I'm giving you my Ramones jacket," I say to the two punks, and look at Louis.

He's already got his off and is dangling it on his index finger.

Because it weighs nothing and is a cheap piece of shit.

"Give it to us or else!" screams the guy with the lead pipe.

"Or else what?" I scream back, really pissed because this jacket means everything to me. It's not just an identity thing, it's my second skin. I'd worn it twenty-four hours a day since Nick and I spent my hard earned bag boy cash on the thing, and there was just simply no way I was parting with it.

They'd have to kill me first. So I told them so.

"No problem," says the guy without the lead pipe. Then he takes out a brown handled switchblade knife and flicks open the long shiny blade.

*

To understand why my motorcycle jacket with the U.S. pins on the hard leather lapels meant so much to me, one has to understand why I purchased the item to begin with.

It was because of the Ramones. A punk rock band that changed my life.

Forever.

*

Sometime in the spring of my junior year, I went to New York with my brothers Sam and Luke, to spend a long weekend relaxing from bagging groceries and getting bagged on by my dad.

My mom and Nick were happy to have us, and it felt good to be away from the Sunshine State, but better to be away from the King and Queen of Water Oak.

They'd been riding up my ass since January about what I was going to do with my life, and when I told them I still had a senior year, they'd just get angrier.

My father kept insisting I start thinking about being an accountant, like he was, and as time went by, it began to stop being a choice. He told me if I didn't follow in his exact footsteps, I'd become a "junkie whore selling myself on the streets of New York" like my mom did. I had no clue what he was talking about, but it didn't sound too good. Or true.

So I was happy to be at Nick and my mom's apartment on West Fourth Street that spring. Away from the pressures of being with my father and stepmother, away from my increasingly stupid sisters, and almost away from myself, the "sorry ass sucking" loser Louis always told me I was.

Also, I was discovering that whatever my father and step-cunt *had* said about my mom and Nick was increasingly untrue. They were the kindest and gentlest people I'd ever met, and I loved them more than words could describe.

But, still, there was that lingering doubt in my head.

The one that kept me tethered to my father like a worn-out volleyball.

And that's probably just how he wanted it.

*

On the second day of our visit, Luke bursts through the glass paneled doors of my mom's apartment on West Fourth Street.

"George," he exclaims, as I'm smoking one of my mom's ultra light shitty cigarettes I'd begged from her a few minutes earlier, "I just saw this fucking movie, and holy fuck if it wasn't fucking you!"

"What the fuck are you fucking talking about you fuck?" I ask my fucking brother.

"Boys," my mom laughs, "language, language, language!"

Her and Nick were cool like that. We could be as potty-mouthed as we wanted, and the more we were, the less we felt like badasses using those sorts of words, which, in the end, was probably my mom's intent.

"It's called fucking *Rock 'n' Roll High School*, and it fucking rocks!" exclaims Luke, in his Disco Sucks T-shirt.

Ten or twenty uses of the word "fuck" later, Luke explains that the movie is playing over at the Eighth Street Playhouse, which is right down the street, a place we go regularly to see *The Rocky Horror Picture Show*.

"Why would I like it?" I ask him.

"Because," he tells me, "it's got that band that you like, the Ramones, in it."

I tell him I only have one recording by them Nick got from the Jefferson Market Library, and although I really do like that "Hey Ho" song, I didn't know about a movie.

It's then my brother gives me a ten dollar bill. Out of his own money.

Money he's earned working odd jobs after school.

"Go see the movie," he says. "It's on me."

"What if I don't like it?" I ask him, not wanting to waste his hard earned money, which I knew I couldn't take anyway, or mine.

"It will change your life," is all he tells me.

Refusing his kind offer, I leave the apartment ten minutes later to catch the next showing.

And my brother is right.

*

When the theater lights dim, and the opening credits of *Rock 'n' Roll High School* flicker upon the screen, I feel my heart start to beat harder. Something was in the air, besides all the pot and cigarette smoke, and that smell of newly purchased leather.

After the first scene where the principal yells at the film's star character, Riff Randell, that's she's worthless and is gonna get detention forever, I start to fall in love.

Here's a girl who's got a bigger mouth then I have, and she digs this group of really ugly guys who play in a punk rock band.

Not only does she like their music, which I find really great myself, she daydreams about sleeping with them.

This beautiful woman.

About a band of guys who are brothers, and wear the coolest uniforms I've ever seen.

See, I was all about the uniforms.

And my brother, Luke, knew that. Of course there were the *Rocky Horror* clothes I sometimes pranced around in, but more often then not, I'd wear a cowboy hat, a construction worker hat, or an Indian headdress around the house or at school. It was all about the Village People for me.

I loved all their tunes, and along with that Dead Boys tape and those *Rocky Horror* albums, it was all I'd ever listen to.

I remember one day Luke telling me the Village People were gay.

"So they're happy, so what?" was my reply.

Luke was kind enough to never burst that bubble.

But now, here I am, watching this movie about this cool rock band and how they help the students not only become cool like them by wearing punk rock motorcycle jackets, but they also help Riff Randell blow the entire school to pieces! And they're funny about it.

Also, the songs were downright hysterical but were played with such a fierce energy and anger that I could not only relate, all I could see was myself up there with them.

And that's when I knew.

First, that I *had* seen these guys before at CBGB with my pals from Greenwich some time ago, and second, that my calling in life was to be a Ramone.

Now I realize that most kids have dreams of growing up to be astronauts, firemen, policemen, stockbrokers, or cross dressing transvestites, and that's all fine and all. But these four guys, in their matching leather jackets and torn blue jeans were my ticket to freedom.

Here was Everyman in his super hero street clothes. And just with the power of a uniform and an electric instrument, he was not only able to score chicks but also to blow up schools, make people dance, and get recognition for being something different.

Something new. To me, anyway.

As I left the Eighth Street Playhouse that day, I felt a surge of energy and anger flow through my veins that felt better than any thing else I had experienced before.

I figured this wasn't going to be that hard. All I'd need was a leather jacket, the same ratty jeans I'd always worn, and my shitted out sneakers, which fit the uniform perfectly.

Like they said in the film, Gabba Gabba One Us!

And that was my big idea.

*

The next day found me wandering around the Lower East Side of New York, looking for the beginning of my transformation from the kid in the worn-out Izod shirts to Ramone.

From boy bagging groceries to boy banging girls. Or at least I thought.

Nick and my mom warned me that leather jackets were *very* expensive, but I told them I had plenty of money saved up in the bank for "college," like my dad had asked me to do. But suddenly, now, this was much more important.

"When we get in the store, George," Nick explains as we set foot on Orchard Street, "act like you really want the motorcycle jacket."

"I do," I say back, with more truth then I've ever spoken again.

"I know you do," says Nick, "but when the guy tells us the price, act disinterested. Like it's too much. We'll haggle and get the jacket cheaper."

Nick was like that. Got everything for cheap. Or didn't get it at all. That morning he'd promised we'd get the leather beast, and, amazingly, I'd still have money in my bank account. But I didn't care. I just wanted to be a Ramone.

"Can't we just do like mom says and buy it?" I ask Nick.

"Barbara doesn't know that these guys will sell you the shirt off their backs," he explains, all knowingly as usual. "They'll come down. But we might have to walk out of the store a few times."

I feel my heart sink. What if it didn't work? What if they wouldn't let us back in?

"Nick, let's just pay them what they want," I plead. "I want a leather jacket. I want to be a Ramone more than anything else in the entire world."

"You'll be a Ramone, George," Nick reassures me. "But please let me haggle. It's my specialty."

So I have no choice but to let Nick do his thing. As painful as this is going to be, at the end of the day I better be a Ramone. Or dead.

It was that serious.

Nick and I walk into a few stores on Orchard Street, and see tons and tons of motorcycle jackets. I try a few on, and look at myself in the mirror.

"Ramone, Georgie Ramone," I whisper under my breath.

And staring back at me in that mirror is finally someone I not only like, but respect. Who I think is cool. Who I would want to be friends with. And it was exciting.

We then hit a few more stores, and finally find one with the perfect jacket. It's made of tough leather, with the right size collar and the exact number of zippers a Ramone should have.

"This is the jacket," I exclaim to Nick, as I model it for him in the store by striking Johnny and Joey and Dee Dee poses. Members of the band.

"Okay, George," says Nick. "It looks perfect. What's the price?"

I look at the tag and tell him. It's over four hundred dollars. Four hundred and seven, to be exact.

But it's a Schott. The best kind made. The official brand of the Ramones.

Nick goes to the sales guy as I stand around there in the jacket, feeling like the king of the world.

"We want this jacket here," says Nick to the guy, "and we ain't gonna pay a lot for it."

"What is the price, sir?" asks the sales guy with a heavy accent I realize to be Yiddish, like the ones some of my grandparents have.

"It says four oh seven, how low you gonna go?" asks Nick.

"If it says four oh seven, it's four oh seven," replies the salesman.

"Up the street they got 'em cheaper. We'll just go there," Nick replies.

"Okay," says the guy. "Four hundred."

"Two fifty," says Nick, in a bold haggling move that makes my intestines hurt.

"No way," says the sales guy. "Three fifty and tax."

They continue to haggle some more and I start to get that feeling of an upcoming diarrhea attack that I usually get when I'm extremely nervous.

What if the guys says no and I don't get the jacket?

Then I'll never be a Ramone. Those US pins we purchased at Weiss & Mahoney earlier that day will go to waste.

"Three hundred plus tax," says the sales guy, "and that's my final offer."

"No tax," Nick replies.

"No way," says the sales guy.

"Okay then, we are leaving," says Nick, and with that, makes me take off the jacket and hang it up back where it belongs. My heart sinks to my torn sneakers.

I start to feel tears well up in my eyes, but I know I'm helpless here. Nick's my stepfather and has been kind to me all his life. If this was the way it went, it was the way it went.

"We are leaving now, George," he says loudly, so the sales guy can hear.

I wish my mom was with us. She'd stop this madman with a plan.

"Bye," says the sales guy as we make our way to the front door.

With tears now running down my face, I feel a real anger toward Nick. Why did he have be such a cheap Jew? Then I realize where the term comes from and get even angrier.

Suddenly, we hear the bell on the door of the store in back of us ring. We turn around and see our sales guy.

"Three hundred, no tax," yells the sales guy. "You're robbing me blind!"

I look at Nick and see a smile crack on his face.

"I told ya so," he says, smiling.

*

Upon returning to the Redneck Riviera, in many ways I feel the old George Tabb is gone. Maybe not forgotten, but certainly on one big fucking vacation.

In his place is someone new, and his name is Georgie Ramone.

He still wears his hair sort of long, but tries straightening it as much as possible. He now wears a Schott Perfecto motorcycle jacket twenty-four hours a day, with the Ramones US pins, and has torn holes in any of his jeans which don't have them, in order to look like his idols: Joey, Johnny, Dee Dee, Marky, and their ex-drummer, Tommy.

The first thing my father says to me when he sees the leather jacket is, "Oh shit!"

And for some reason, it made me smile. Big time.

He then tells me that when he was in high school, the bad kids, called greasers, wore those jackets. They were the types of guys who rode motorcycles, and who my mother, the whore, had dated before he saved her.

When I ask him what he wore he tells me all about his letter jackets. The kinds the jocks wear with the school's logo on them.

I explain to him that this jacket is me, and he asks me if I think I'm the Fonz from *Happy Days* or something.

Cybill, walking into the living room during this conversation, takes one look at me, and her jaw drops. And for the first time, she's speechless.

I think about what my father just asked, and it is a very good question. Am I Fonzie from *Happy Days*?

"Sure I'm like the Fonz," I tell my dad, and stepmother, who's still speechless. "He's the coolest besides the Ramones, so why not?"

Then my father asks me about the Ramones and I show him the T-shirt I'm wearing under my new leather jacket. It's a Ramones one.

"Ra-Mone-ees?" he asks.

I explain it's pronounced "Ra-Mones."

He asks me who they are and I explain they are the coolest band ever, and one day I'm going to be in the band with them.

Cybill, finally able to speak, mumbles something inaudible to both myself and my father.

"Speak up, woman!" demands the King of Water Oak.

"I can't believe it," Cybill almost whispers. "He actually looks good!"

"Take it off," my father suddenly demands.

"Why?" I say in a snotty tone, one that Georgie Ramone would use.

"Because you'll never make a good accountant looking like a thug," my father yells.

"You know what?" my jacket and I say to my father. "Fuck you and your Black Wing #2 pencils. Why don't you shove them up your ass!"

Cybill laughs under her breath and I wink at her. Like the Fonz.

"Why you little pussy," my father starts, and he lunges toward me.

With strength and a sense of confidence I didn't even know I possessed, I grab my father's right arm, which is in the direct path of my face, quickly bend it at the elbow, and force it behind his back.

Then I push it up.

Hard.

"What the fuck do you think you're doing?" screams my father, purple with rage and shaking worse than his father, my grandfather, who has Parkinson's.

"Don't fuck with Georgie Ramone," I say to the old man. "Don't you ever fuck with Georgie Ramone."

Not keeping my eye on Cybill, I miss the fact she's grabbed a brass fire poker from near the fire place, and the next thing I know I wake up with a bloody bump on my forehead.

But it was worth it.

*

Back at Leon High School, suddenly I'm not looked at like the Two Million Dollar Jew with the bionic arm, but like something else.

I ask Mr. Bott, my psych. teacher, what he thinks, and he tells me it's probably because I look like James Dean or Marlon Brando. Two names I've never heard before. He tells me to look them up.

I also tell Mr. Bott about the Ramones, and how I've finally found my calling in life. He then asks the first important question I hadn't thought of.

What instrument are you going to play in the band?

Doh.

Months and months later, I decide upon the guitar.

But not before every kid in school steers very clear of me, and I take to sitting in the back of the classroom, dozing off whenever I feel like it because the teachers are too scared to say anything, and I'm really fucking exhausted from my full-time bag boy job after school.

Things continue as they are, with my mom and Nick buying me all the Ramones albums to date, as well as another one by the Dead Boys and music from some other cool bands they think I'd like, like the Clash and the Jam.

I instantly fall in love with the Jam's "Batman Theme," and soon, Louis, Scott, and I are driving around the Leon parking lot blasting it from the Orange Batmobile.

The jocks look at us with anger and fear.

The preppy kids just hold their noses even higher in the air, except for a few of the girls who can't help but get all bleary eyed, and we are the kings of the freaks. Scott and Louis get all the pot they could ever want to smoke, and we are invited to all the cool stoner parties.

And I have fun at them. Especially the one where I met Crystal.

*

One late spring or early summer evening, which is about the same thing in Florida, I went to a keg party with Louis and Scott and Tommy Corn in the Orange Batmobile. As we pull into the front of the house where we hear all sorts of wild screams over the Ramones' *Rocket to Russia* album, I park the car, and we make our way toward the action.

At first, everyone just stares at my friends like they didn't belong, but when they see me behind them, in my ripped jeans, Ramones T-shirt, and shiny black leather jacket with the US pins on, they quickly change their tune and welcome us with open arms.

"That jacket really is amazing," says Tommy, as we make our way toward the keg, with huge plastic cups in hand. "It's like magic or something."

I tell him I know, and Tommy asks where he can get one.

We drink until Scott gets loosened up to the point where he tells us about his overweight woman fetish, and we nod like we care, having heard this from him every time he's had a few too many drinks.

Then, out of the corner of my eye, I see her.

She's wearing a purple tube top, and her breasts defy gravity. She's got long straight brown hair I find myself jealous of, and eyes as blue as the stripes on my Nike All Court sneakers, the official footwear of the Ramones.

I quickly catch her looking me back in the eyes, and glance toward the ground.

"What's wrong Tabb you sorry ass sucker?" asks Louis.

I ask Louis to look over at the girl with the long brown hair, and see if she's looking at me.

"You mean the one with the huge titties?" he asks.

Furiously, I tell him not to talk about the love of my life like that, and just to fucking look and see if she's looking toward us.

"Yup," says Louis, "she is."

Then I get confused.

I wonder what I'm supposed to do next?

Do I walk up to her and say something, or will that make me look like an asshole?

Should I play hard to get?

Should I send Scott over to see if she likes me?

Lost in thought, Tommy Corn interrupts me by clearing his throat.

"Tabb," says Tommy Corn, God's Gift to Women, "looks like you got the fishin' for pussy blues."

"Huh?" I ask my pal who today looks more like a toned-down Jerry Lewis than the *Nutty Professor* one he usually looks like. He still smells like a gorilla though.

I tell him I don't know what to say to that beautiful girl over there, who I nod to with my chin.

"The one with the big titties?" he asks, "Tabb, my man, you've got good taste. But that doesn't mean you taste good!"

And with that, he cracks himself up.

I'm not amused.

"Look," says God's Gift to Women, after calming himself down, "just go over to her and introduce yourself. She'll like you for who you are. Plus, you'll look confident. Chicks dig confidence."

I take Tommy's advice and three minutes later, I've got a date for the next night.

*

Crystal and I decide it will be fun to hang out with Scott, and his on-again, off-again girlfriend, Cindy.

We all decide to chip in on the best bottle of wine we can afford, and as we sit in Scott's mom's apartment, with her away for the weekend, we sip away at the Boone's Hill grape-flavored alcohol.

"This sure is a good vintage," says Scott, as he holds up the bottle and everyone laughs.

But me.

I think it is a good vintage.

Whatever that means.

After more drinking, Scott and Cindy tell us they are going upstairs to Scott's room for "some action," and we should do the same on the living room couch.

Crystal says that's a good idea, and suddenly she lays on her back and tells me to climb on top of her.

I do.

Leather jacket and all.

"You look so hot in that jacket," Crystal tells me. "I want you!"

Those words bounce off my brain's walls and echo over and over again.

"I want you."

No one has ever said that to me. I never knew anyone could feel that way about me.

So I tell her I want her as well, and the next thing I know our tongues are pogoing, and my hands, which are beneath her back, slowly climb toward those two Mount Everests.

I touch her breasts softly at first, and Crystal lets out a small sigh in a high pitch that sounds like Heaven to me.

So I kiss her harder, and begin to rub her nipples around in tiny circles like Scott always tells me he does with "his women."

She sighs again, and then, to my shock, removes her shirt, and forces my face between the nicest boobies I've ever seen.

With my nose pressed hard against her chest, and each side of my mouth only able to inhale soft flesh, I start to suffocate.

Finally I have to pull away roughly to get some air.

"Are you okay?" coos Crystal, whose hands are busy touching and stroking my leather jacket.

"Fine," I say, not knowing what to do next.

Thankfully, she helps me.

"What do they taste like?" Crystal asks.

"Huh?" I say, totally confused.

"My boobs, what do they taste like?" she asks.

I tell her I don't know.

"Well, find out, silly," she says, and pushes my curly head into her huge mounds once more.

I lick and lick and then lick some more.

"Suck them," Crystal quietly whispers in my ear.

I do as I'm told, not wanting to get yelled at.

As I feel one of her hard round nipples in my mouth I suddenly start to think of my mom.

And how I used to do the same thing with her when I was a tiny baby.

She'd hold me in my favorite blue blanket, and I knew I'd never feel safer than I was right then.

As I suck harder and harder, Crystal's voice washes me away from my thoughts.

"Well? she asks.

"Well what?" I whisper.

"My tits, do you taste the coconut?" she asks.

I wonder what in the hell she's talking about, and then she begins to explain to me that she had purchased coconut butter oil to wear out in the sun, and that most men found it very tasty.

So I told her I agreed with "most men."

Even though I couldn't taste a thing.

Except love.

The next thing I know Crystal's let go of my Ramones jacket and has positioned her hand over my crotch.

And it's as hard as a rock.

She starts to rub it hard, and, of course, I get the worse feeling of a diarrhea attack I've ever had, quickly excuse myself, and run into Scott's bathroom where I spend the next fifteen minutes cursing my lousy stomach and worse luck.

When I return to Crystal, she's completely dressed, and asks me if I will drive her home.

As I do so in the Orange Batmobile, we hardly talk.

"You don't like me," she says, "do you?"

I tell her I do, and that my stomach just hurt really bad.

"Sure," says Crystal, "you just think I'm a dummy like everyone else does!"

I tell her I truly don't and that I'd really love to see her again.

"When?" she asks.

"Tomorrow," I tell her.

She thinks about it for minute, then tells me the day after tomorrow would be better.

I should have listened to her.

*

The next night I show up at Crystal's dorm on the Florida State University campus. I park the the Orange Batmobile and take the bouquet of flowers I purchased for the new love of my life out of the back seat.

As I climb the stairs of her dorm, to the room she left me at the night before after giving me the best French kiss ever, I figure I'm going to surprise her. And when she sees the flowers, she'll just fall as in love with me as I am with her.

When I get to her door with the neon rainbow stickers and pictures of David Cassidy on it, I softly knock.

No answer.

So I knock harder.

Still, no answer.

So being the jerk I am, I slowly turn the door knob to see if the door is locked. If it isn't, I figure I'll just leave the flowers on her bed as a surprise, and leave a really nice note.

The handle turns and I slowly open the door into her dorm room which seems to be only lit with candles.

"Who's that?" I hear Crystal's voice whisper, as she shuffles around in her bed.

My eyes try to adjust to the darkness, and finally I see the shape of my love's head on her pillow.

"It's me, George," I say as smoothly as I can.

"George who?" she asks.

There's more shuffling in the bed.

"George you went out with last night," I say, sort of annoyed.

"The guy with the leather jacket?" she asks, as I can make more and more of her out. She's now sitting up in bed, totally topless, and she's hitting something under the sheets between her legs.

"Same George," I say.

"Now is not a good time," she starts to tell me, then throws her head back and moans like Linda Blair in *The Exorcist*.

"What the fuck?" I start to say, then see some guy's head pop up from under the sheets and look directly at me.

"Who the fuck are you?" says the guy, who I can see is clearly older than me, what with his full mustache and all.

In shock, I take the flowers I have in my left hand like a dumb ass and throw them toward the couple in bed.

Then, without a word, I turn around and leave the room.

I hear them laughing hysterically as I close the door behind me, but it just bounces off my leather jacket, and I don't feel a thing.

I'm a Ramone.

And Ramones don't get hurt.

*

Throughout the rest of that school year, my summer, then the start of my senior year, it's clear that my leather jacket becomes more to me than just an item of clothing. Somehow I wrap my identity and self into its wonderful quilted layers, and hard leather exterior.

It *is* me.

*

So there I am, a few months later, freezing and with the taste of blood in my mouth, as I stare at a streetlight's reflection on the blade of a brown handled knife in some guy's hand.

"So what's it gonna be, eh?" asks the guy with the knife as Louis hands his fake-ass leather jacket over to the guy with the lead pipe, who is too stupid to know the weight is totally wrong.

Full of rage, and not to be robbed of my leather jacket, never mind of *who* I am, I give him the answer he doesn't expect to hear.

"You'll have to kill me first," I hear myself say.

No fucking way this guy is taking everything I've got away from me by stealing this jacket. No way this fucker is taking the respect I've earned, and my desire and life's goal to be in the Ramones. No way, no how, never.

"Suit yourself, amigo," says the guy and the last thing I remember before waking up in a pile of snow five minutes later is Louis's girlie shriek.

As I stand up, dizzy, out of the red snow I've been laying in, I look down at my Sid Vicious shirt and see it's covered with blood. I look at Louis, who's got his arms wrapped around himself, freezing, who keeps asking if I'm okay.

I feel my head and face and find it sticky.

I'm covered in blood.

Then I feel my chest and it's not there.

The leather jacket, that is.

My Ramones leather jacket.

And I'm pissed.

"I tried to tell you not to resist, Tabb," explains Louis, and I tell him to can it.

"You fucking pussy," I yell at my best friend. "You let them take my jacket."

"I couldn't stop them," yells Louis, and then I see the tears he's been trying to hide from me travel down his face.

We make our way home in the icy weather, unable to find a cab, and by the time we get home, my blood has frozen into icicles that are dripping from my face.

My mom, waiting up for us, faints.

*

The next day, after filling out a police report where the cops just laugh at Louis and I, Nick, against my say-so, buys me another leather jacket. In fact, the same make and model.

But I won't take it.

I tell him I've been robbed of everything, even of my security, and I don't want that to ever happen again.

He just hands me a pair of US pins to go with the new Ramones leather jacket and tells me to think about it.

I do and take neither the jacket nor the pins.

*

About a month later, while visiting Nick's mom in Florida, my mom and stepfather give me the new leather jacket again. After briefly protesting, they explain I can't be a Ramone without one, and I see their point.

*

When I put the new one on, it feels as old and as familiar as my first one.

And I start to cry.

Looking at my mom and Nick, they just smile and swear they'll never tell a soul.

And they never did.

WE WANT YOU!

IT WAS DECIDED at the start of my senior year that I'd double up on all my classes for the first half of the school year and graduate early.

That conclusion not only came from my stepmother and father, but myself as well. The summer before had been hellish at best, and I knew my survival rate living with the King and Queen of Water Oak was lowering every time I set foot in their house.

At one point in August, Lester and Cybill had sent me away to live with her sister's kids in the suburbs of San Francisco.

Being the idiot in the leather jacket I was, I should have just gone straight to my mom and Nick's, but there still was that issue of trust, and my father and Cybill played their cards beautifully.

That was until I found out from my Aunt Helen after a couple of weeks why I wasn't allowed to drive the family car, and couldn't be trusted around their kids, who were exactly the same age as my brothers and I.

"What's up?" I finally ask my stepmother's sister and husband Don.

I've done nothing wrong, and me and my Ramones leather jacket were getting along fine with my cousins Marc, Bruce, Daniel, and Michael.

We had good times in Lake Tahoe and better times with Marc driving us up and down El Camino Real, "cruising for chicks," which, of course, we never found.

"What do you mean?" asks my Aunt Helen, as Uncle Don nods in agreement.

"Look," I say, "I know it's not my leather jacket or the fact that I've turned your kids onto the punk rock. That was going to happen eventually anyway."

They're silent.

Finally, with her eyes gazing at the floor my Aunt Helen tells me the truth of why I'm living with her and her family. And why I was to begin school out there in just a few weeks.

"It's because you are using," explains my Aunt Helen.

"Yes," says Uncle Don, "we know all about it."

"Using what?" I ask, sincerely.

"You know," says Aunt Helen. "I don't think we have to explain it to you."

But I insisted she does. I had no idea what "using" meant, but it didn't sound good from the tones in their voices. And if that's what kept their kids at least a yard's length away from me most of the time, I needed to know.

"Heroin," Uncle Don finally sighs in their pleasant Hillsborough living room.

I look at them in shock.

There was that word again, which I knew now to be some sort of awful drug I'd never even seen, never mind tried.

"Where'd you hear that?" I ask, trying to keep from flying into a blind rage, and smashing all their family belongings. Happy pictures of the boys and their parents, trophies for their achievements, and nice little knickknacks the kids had made for their parents that were actually kept around as memoirs. Actually, I was sort of jealous.

"Your father and Cybill told us," my Aunt Helen explains, "but don't worry, your secret is safe with us."

Uncle Don just nods his head in agreement.

I look at the two of them, genuinely nice people, especially to take in a "heroin addict" like myself, and don't know where to start.

So I start from the beginning.

I explain to my stepmother's sister that I only smoked pot five times before I died, that I didn't do drugs, and, more than anything, I wanted to be like my heroes the Ramones, Spider-Man, Captain Kirk, and James Bond.

I wanted to do good things in the world, and heroin wasn't one of them.

Upon hearing this, the surprising thing was they didn't go into shock.

Or denial.

In fact, it was Uncle Don who spoke first.

"I knew your sister was a lying bitch," he says flat out, flooring even me.

"Don!" Aunt Helen exclaims, then sadly, acknowledging what he'd said, shakes her head in agreement.

"I knew she was a liar since she was twelve," my Aunt Helen says more to herself then to anyone else in the room.

I say nothing.

Finally Uncle Don speaks. "So what are we to do?" he asks.

I just shrug my shoulders, feeling like I'm drowning in a pile of horse shit, and there is no escape.

"We call his real mother," my Aunt Helen says, and with that asks me for her and Nick's number, then dials it.

Standing there in shock, I listen as she, for the first time, talks to my real mother and finds her to be as charming and as wonderful as I do.

When she finally hangs up the phone it's been decided that I'm going to live with my real mother and Nick, and that they, Aunt Helen and Uncle Don, are so sorry for ever believing Cybill and her megalomaniacal husband, Lester.

Those are their words, not mine.

When I honestly tell them the fears my father and Cybill have installed in me about my mom and Nick being junkies and selling me on the streets of New York, they finally shine a flashlight onto the darkest part of my worst fears and expose them for what they really are.

Head games.

And lies.

They explain that my father has always been a "power player," whatever that means, and that he likes to twist people around his fat little fingers by toying with their brains.

While all of this didn't make much sense, what did is the explanation of my mother's and Nick's real love for me from the mouth of Cybill's sister.

So, thanking them for all they had done, I moved in with my mom and Nick for what I thought was for good.

*

A week before my senior year was to begin in New York, where my mom and Nick have registered me at a local high school in Greenwich Village, the phone rings and I answer it.

It's my father.

He explains to me that he's really sorry about what happened in California and all, and wants me to come home to Tallahassee to finish out my senior year of high school.

When I tell him to go fuck himself, he tells me he's a "new man," has been seeing a shrink, and now understands all the bad things he's done, and wants to make things up to me.

I tell him I'll call him back and hang up the phone.

With a twinge of guilt in my voice, I explain to my mom and Nick, who are happier than they've ever been in their lives to have a son of theirs living with them, that my father wants me back in Floriduh.

While they tell me they won't stand in my way, they do say it's a bad idea and that a person's change doesn't overnight. I tell them it can, especially with my leather jacket and all, and my mom wisely tells me I'm just becoming who've I've always been.

But, feeling guilty, and bad for my father, who has seemed to make a real effort to try and love me again, I make the tragic mistake of taking him up on his offer and fly back to the Redneck Riviera.

As Barbara, Nick, and I stand at New York's Kennedy Airport, I hug them with tears in my eyes, and thank them for all they've done.

"We'll see you soon, honey," my mom whispers into my ear, and I can feel her tears against my cheek.

Nick then just shakes my hand and can't look me in the eyes.

*

At the Tallahassee airport, on the other end of my trip, my father greets me a half hour late. After throwing my belongings into the back of his pickup truck, he drives us back to the plantation. On the way, he explains that he's the stud of Northern Florida, and "fucks" like five or six women a week that he picks up at a bar in the Timberlane Mall called the Watering Hole.

When I ask him why he's telling me this, he tells me he just wants to be "honest," like his shrink has told him to be.

I feel like asking him to turn around and drive me back to the airport, but I am too much of a pussy.

*

So it's decided I'll double up on my classes my senior year and get the fuck out of Tara as quick as I can.

Of course, within the first week of being back on the land of mighty fences I helped build, my father introduces me to his new best friend.

A shovel.

It greets me in my face, hard, after I get home late from work one night from Publix.

After icing down my nose so my eyes won't turn too black, I ask my father about "the new deal" he had promised me on the phone in New York, and this whole honesty and shrink thing.

"I changed my mind," my father replies.

"Oh," I say, knowing I'm fucked.

*

"Mr. Tabb," says some hard looking man with a crew cut and a full army uniform in the office of my school's guidance counselor, "I hear you are interested in joining the United States Armed Forces!"

I do a double take.

A few minutes earlier, the school's guidance counselor, who looked like a female Nutty Professor, had called me into her office.

I was happy to go as taking Algebra I for the third time in a row was getting quite boring.

"George," the wild-eyed, gray haired, witchy woman had said to me, "today you are going to have a visitor that your father and I arranged."

When I asked her why, she told me it was because of my PSAT scores.

Some test that helps determine what college you get into.

I remembered taking it a few weeks back, and forming the word "Ramones" with those tiny little bubbles on the answer sheet, thinking it was a masterpiece.

Obviously they didn't.

So GI Joe walks into the Wicked Witch of the South's office and greets me by saluting like they do in movies.

I salute him back, then say, "Heil Myself," straight out of Mel Brooks *The Producers*.

GI Joe just looks at me funny, and I see his kung-fu grip start to tighten.

"Nice Air Force pins ya got there, soldier," says G.I. Joe.

"Huh?" I ask the man who looks more like a football player than what I imagined a real-life soldier really looked like.

"There, on that hippie jacket," he explains, "those are official United States Air Force pins!"

I explain they are *also* the pins the Ramones wear on their leather jackets, and the Ramones are the coolest band ever.

"Do they play that rock 'n' roll music?" he asks, in all seriousness.

I nod my head and feel like I'm back in some fifties movie, or better yet, Rock 'n' Roll High School. And I'm Riff Randell!

"Well," says the army guy, "we at the USMC think the fly boys are a bunch of pussies, but that's just our opinion," he continues, laughing to himself.

"USMC?" I have to ask.

"That's United States Marine Corps," GI Joe yells at me. "And if anyone can make you a man, it's us!"

I look at the guy and think of Dr. Frank-N-Furter from *Rocky Horror*. He tried making someone a man, too. And look what happened to him.

"Sorry," I say. "I'm not interested."

"But George," says my guidance counselor, as she looks ready to zoom off on her broom, "you don't really have a choice. Your grades on the PSATs are so low, the only place you can go after you finish school this year *is* the military."

GI Joe just bites his upper lip.

"You mean to tell me," I scream, now pissed that I'm put in this retarded position not by from the smelly woman to my right, but by my father, "that my straight As don't mean shit?"

"But you got 'fives' after each A!" exclaims the Witch.

I then think about the school's grading system and remember they put numbers after each grade to show the amount of effort a student puts in.

Most kids got A1s or E5s.

That made sense.

But I got A5s because, number one, I didn't give a shit and slept through class, and secondly the tests were so easy that taking them was like filling in coloring books with pretty colors. Where I liked to draw outside the lines.

"You have no self discipline, and the United States Marines Corps will change that!" GI Joe suddenly screams at me, taking charge of the room.

"Fuck you," I say to the army guy, even though he does have a huge weapon attached to his hip. "I'm a Ramone, and we don't listen to nobody."

"You see!" shouts the guidance counselor.

"Ramone?" yells GI Joe. "What, are you? Some sort of Mexican?"

I calmly explain to him I'm a Jew, and besides having bionic arms, and specially cut penises, we just don't do grunt work.

With that the guy gets furious and grabs me by my hard leather lapels. He almost makes one of my U.S. pins pop off.

"Hands off the jacket, jerk-off," I say to the marine, whose face is now turning purple with rage, just like my father's.

I realize I'm beginning to enjoy myself in a very sick sort of way.

"No tickey, no laundry," I say.

G.I. Joe, probably angrier than when he found out he had no wiener when he tried to have sex with Barbie, who's also missing some parts, slams the desk in front of me.

"You fucking little shit," he screams at the top of his lungs. "You aren't anywhere near USMC quality!"

"Good," I tell the purple man in the green suit. "So that means you'll leave now?"

The guy, shaking uncontrollably, leaves the guidance counselor's office without saying a word.

As the Witch and I watch him walk down the school's hallway, he kicks over every chair he can find.

Some tables set up for a bake sale, too.

"Well," I say to the gray haired woman off to my right, "that went well, huh?"

*

That night my dad wakes me up around three in the morning with an ax in his hand.

My hand is still down my pajama pants, and an issue of Playboy is laid out on the bed next to me, sticky.

He grabs me by my hard leather lapels with his right hand, and shows me the ax with his left.

I look at the wood handled wonder, with the bright red paint on the metal near the blade, then quickly move my free hand to my penis as well.

"You little shit," my father screams at the top of his lungs. "Do you even know how bad you made me look today?"

He's screaming so loud that suddenly I see my brothers and sisters at my bedroom door, looking in at the maniac with the ax, and his son, in bed with his leather jacket on with his hands protecting his dick for dear life.

"Sorry Dad," is all I can manage to say.

"Sorry?" my father yells. "You think you're sorry?"

I nod my head, not knowing what else to say.

"I'll show you sorry," my father screams and lifts the ax above his head.

It's at this point I see my sisters and brothers break into tears.

All of them.

They are scared to death and suddenly I don't feel anything for myself, but everything for them.

They were witnessing this obscenity. It would damage their minds forever, and if I were to die, I don't know how they could live with it.

"Look at your kids," I yell at my father as he turns from plum to purple to dark blue, shaking with rage.

He sees Luke, Sam, Diana, Teresa, and Stephanie all bawling their eyes out.

Then he looks at me and the ax.

"Jesus Christ," he says to himself as he slowly lowers the ax. "What did I almost do?"

Everyone gets quiet as my dad climbs off me and slowly makes his way toward the door, where my siblings have gathered.

They begin to walk away and through his gritted teeth my father seethes, "I should have just shot you. It'd have been much easier."

*

So as one could imagine, my senior year at Leon High School was uncomfortable at best. Even though I'd doubled up on my classes, I still found myself having plenty of free time, which I shared with the bottles of Mad Dog 20/20 and Thunderbird I kept in my school locker. I realize I must have smelled drunk most of the time, but no one seemed to care. And any teacher who did, after meeting my father, got strangely quiet.

*

My senior year ended with a fizzle right before Christmas vacation. I'd taken all the courses I thought I needed to get my high school degree and was already accepted into the University of Florida for the spring semester.

Which was a good thing, because, after my first few months at college, I found out I was short a couple of PE credits and was asked to return to Leon High for some summer courses to receive my high school diploma.

Which, of course, I never did.

GOD'S GIFT TO WOMEN

"COLLEGE IS ALL ABOUT THE PUSSY," Tommy Corn explains to me as I bag groceries during that lull between the end of my senior year and the beginning of college at the University of Florida in Gainesville.

The start of my freshman year had been pushed back to March, which is fine with me.

It meant I could work double shifts and have enough money to survive when I finally did start school. I could have started the winter quarter in January, but I just didn't think my head was in the right place yet.

Nor was my wallet.

My father had said he'd help pay for *some* of my college education, but he expected me to work for most of it, which was fine by me.

So I took as many hours at Publix during those few months as I could, and Tommy Corn and I got to be great pals.

"Pussy and more pussy," Tommy explains as he bags groceries beside me. He's supposed to be in the back, counting cans of peaches or pineapples or something, but I can tell he is in the mood to be social. His hair is actually combed almost into a style that made sense, and he's wearing his new glasses, the ones with the wire rims, which make him look less like Jerry Lewis and more like a professor or something.

But he still stinks like a gorilla.

"You know, Tommy," I say, as I put a bottle of spaghetti sauce and a can of powdered milk on top of someone's Wonder Bread, "I think I'm getting really close."

"Really?" asks God's Gift to Women.

I tell Tommy that since Louis and Scott have been away at college and I've been on my own with my leather jacket, which Henry, my floor manager, is nice enough to let me wear at work, along with my clip-on tie, that I've started to really "score" with the chicks.

"Score?" asks Tommy. "How?"

I explain to him about the more than five times I've french kissed girls and even about feeling Scott's girlfriend's boobies at a movie theater because Scott said it was okay.

"He's fine with you fiddling around with her fun-bags?" he yells, and suddenly the front of the store gets very quiet.

After a nasty look from my mean cashier that tells us we're talking too loud, we bring it down a notch. Or five.

"She lets you touch her titties?" Tommy whispers, asking the same question again.

I explain that Scott told me it would be good practice, and besides, he really didn't like her all that much anymore. He was on to bigger and better things.

But mostly bigger.

"Were they firm like ripe cantaloupes," asks Tommy, "or soft like Ziploc bags full of water?"

I look at Tommy Corn and wonder where the hell he comes up with this stuff.

*

During these months, I also begin to hang out a lot with my brother, Luke. He's never really around Water Oak Plantation, but for that matter, neither am I.

Luke's opened his own pinball parlor at the Timberlane Mall, next to my father's favorite watering hole, and between breaks at work, or before or after, I go by his shop to visit.

And play pinball.

Lots of it.

Luke's place is stylin'. He's got all the great Gottleib machines from the fifties and the newer ones like Xenon and even Playboy, which is hardly ever *not* being played.

Plus, Luke's raking in the dough, and I'm happy for him.

Happy because I know money flows through his hands like water, and whatever he's going to do with his life, it's going to involve lots of cash. So this is a great start for my kid brother.

Plus, he tells me it keeps him away from the Munsters, his nickname for the kind folks over at Water Oak Plantation.

One day, while I'm busy turning over Aces High for a second time on one quarter, we see my father park his truck in front of the bar next door.

We both look at our watches and realize it's just after one in the afternoon.

Ten minutes later, he walks out with a blonde girl who can't be much more than two years older than either of us, and we seethe.

*

A week later, when I invite Sally from *Rocky Horror* over to see my Ramones record collection at the mansion, my dad, who is supposed to be out banging one of my schoolmates, is sitting in the kitchen, reading the *Wall Street Journal*.

"The market's gone to shit," he mumbles as Sally and I walk in the side door.

I try to ignore him and sneak Sally past him from behind, but he obviously sees us, then opens his mouth.

"George," he says, "aren't you going to introduce me to your friend here?"

"Um," I stammer. "Oh yeah. Dad, this is Sally. Sally, this is my father."

"Nice to meet you," Sally says as she says sticks out her hand to shake my father's.

My dad, being the gentleman he is, grabs Sally's hand, gets on one knee, and kisses it.

Sally nervously laughs while I get angry.

"Well," I say, grabbing Sally by the waist, "that's that. See ya later, dad!"

"Not so fast," says my father, who pushes my arm away from Sally's midsection.

"We're gonna listen to some Ramones and *Rocky Horror*," I explain to my father, "you know, the music you *hate*."

"Can I ask you something?" my father says in a tone to Sally that's more of a demand.

"Um," stammers Sally, who begins to blush, "sure."

I'm thinking he's going to ask her about college or why she likes *Rocky Horror*, or what's with the bright red dyed hair.

But what falls out of his mouth next is something I'd never thought I'd hear.

"Why are you hanging out with my son?" he asks. "Are you having sex with him?"

Being a virgin, his question stabs me so hard in the chest I wish for instant death. Right then and there.

Sally, who knows that my dad is a shit from all the stories I've told her, stands and looks at him in utter disbelief.

"What?" says my father, on the verge of laughing. "You're not fucking him? I don't blame you."

Sally says nothing as I glance toward the rack of cutting knives a few feet from my left hand, one of which is about to go through my father's head.

"Listen, Sally," my dad says, "you shouldn't be dating or hanging out with losers like my son. He's got no goals in life except to be a worthless musician, and his dick is tiny."

I can't believe I hear what's coming out of his mouth and am in too much shock to do anything. Let alone grab a kitchen knife.

"You should be dating someone like me," my father continues, "and ignore useless cock suckers like my unwanted offspring."

Getting up the nerve to grab the knife and splatter his brains all over my leather jacket, I finally find my left hand inching toward a black handled knife that's going through his black heart any second now.

"You know what?" screams Sally, shocking the both of us. "George told me you were a piece of crap and all these wild stories about you. But I never believed him!"

"And now?" asks my father, arrogantly.

"You're lower than anything George even remotely described," she yells, almost in tears. "And on top of that, his cock is huge!"

My father stares at Sally, stunned.

The next thing I know she's all over him, trying to claw out his eyes, and pulling huge chunks of curly hair from his big stupid head.

"I'm gonna fuckin' kill you," yells Sally, as tears now pour out of her eyes. "I'm going to rip you to shreds!"

I manage to drag Sally off my father before he does anything dumb like killing her.

As I drag Sally to my room, hysterical, I look back at my father, who, more than anything, looks confused.

*

I tell this whole story to Tommy Corn the next day at Publix, and he tells me it's a good thing I'm going away to college soon.

"You guys are on a crash course with death," he explains, while we play hooky from doing anything productive and drink stolen bottles of Grolsch in the store's cement loading area.

Suddenly out from behind some wooden crates that hide a secret back door to Henry's office, our boss joins us.

We immediately stop talking, and try to hide our beers as best we can.

Down our pants.

Henry laughs and tells us to feel free and drink. That he's just done a few shots of Wild Turkey in his office.

We look at our boss with the horseshoe print in his forehead and realize just how cool he is.

"Ya know," slurs Henry, who must have overheard everything we were saying, "I hear lots of people calling me retarded behind my back."

We look at him, then the ground. Feeling rotten.

"Oh no," he slurs, "not you fine boys. Them awful customers."

We nod our heads, not knowing what else to do.

"Well," continues Henry, "it seems to me the biggest retard of them all has got to be your father, George."

And with that, he puts his arm around me.

So I put my arm around him.

Then Henry says something that Tommy Corn and I never thought we'd hear from our boss.

"Hey, Tommy," he says, "why don't you run into my office and open the top right drawer. I got half a bottle of Wild Turkey in there, and I think the three of us should finish it off!"

*

The rest of the day at work is spent with smiles on our faces, and the warmth of Wild Turkey in our hearts.

Then, soon, college begins.

AT THE CROSSROADS

SO, THERE I AM, after my first week of college, sitting on this overly hard wooden bench, with my left testicle stuck to my right thigh under my ripped blue jeans. With the heat more than unbearable, I find it downright disgusting that I literally have my underwear in a twist.

While it's true the air conditioning is blasting at full force, it does nothing for me and my leather jacket. We both feel like we're going to faint.

As I sit there, in the Cross Roads Church of Christ, I watch as some of my new friends take the stage in front of us all. We have gathered together that night to celebrate something about birth. I have trouble remembering what the exact words this hippie looking guy who led the church had told us, but it had something to do with Jesus Christ, something about being a shellfish, and most importantly, my addiction to masturbation.

"Brothers and sisters," starts this Charles Manson look-alike, as me and about a hundred other "lost" students fidget around in our seats. The word "lost" is the church's, not ours.

"We have gathered here tonight to witness the rebirth of some of your fellow human beings," Charles Christ continues, "and tonight we have someone very special."

I wonder who the special guest star could be as my brain floats in the steam bath being inhaled through my nose and mouth. Bob Barker?

"We have a Jew!" exclaims Jesus Manson.

I look around at everyone else in the room to see someone with curly hair and a big nose like mine, and it's then I realize that everyone is staring at me.

"His name is George," explains the good preacher, "and tonight, this very special night, he shall be reborn!"

It all sounds very *Rocky Horror* to me, and I can't wait to see the glass tank full of colored liquids and all those lights blinking on and off.

Of course I'm oblivious to the fact that what was about to happen has nothing to do with making a blonde haired man with a tan, but everything to do with buying real estate in my brain and scoring some kind of bizarre brownie points.

But let me back up a bit.

*

After my father drops me off at Graham Hall on the University of Florida campus, I lug all my crap to what turns out to be my first dorm room. My father, telling me he has no time to move stuff, because he's a busy man, just leaves me and my pile of belongings on the curb outside the dorm, wishes me luck, then speeds off into the hot Gainesville sun.

Once I get my clothes, my books, and most important, my new Sears stereo system and record collection into the tiny closet that tries to pass as a double room, I have a good look around.

On what I assume to be my side of the room I see a cot with what looks like a very uncomfortable mattress on it. I probably thought that because of the springs poking through the top of it.

Other then that, that side of the room appears to be empty.

But the other side, the one near the basement window that faces the cement wall, which makes the place feel like a womb with a view, were some strange belongings that should have set off bells and alarms in my head. But after living with my monster of a father for the last eighteen years, alarms in my mind were either nonexistent, or worse, set only to go off when guilt settled in.

Anyway, hanging behind a nicely made bed with a mattress that looked ten times more comfortable than mine is a huge confederate flag, with the words "The South will rise again" written across the bottom.

As I stare at the fucking thing, hoping like hell my roommate isn't some whiskey drinking redneck, who uses the word "nigger" in every other sentence, I'm zapped from my thoughts from a familiar voice behind me.

"So, what do ya think, Tabb?" asks Louis, my bag boy buddy.

Seeing my pal with the owl shaped glasses and wavy brown hair, I can't help but drop everything, run to the door, and give him the biggest hug I can.

"Get off me you sorry ass sucker," says Louis, as he hugs me back even tighter.

I'd spoken to Louis the evening before and told him when I would be arriving. And where.

Having been at the college a whole two quarters before me, Louis, with his zero point zero grade point average, told me over the phone that he hoped like hell that I'd take some classes he could go with me to. As it turns out he's very shy. To the point of not wanting to go anywhere alone. Hence the nonexistent grades.

I felt sorry for him and hoped like hell I could crack him out of his shell.

Seeing him in his new fake leather jacket, I can tell he is already on his way.

*

After unpacking some of my shit, mainly the Sears stereo and a few Ramones albums, Louis and I dance around my new room to songs like "Sheena Is a Punk Rocker" and "Suzy Is a Headbanger," then play air guitar to "Teenage Lobotomy" and "Today Your Love, Tomorrow the World."

While we are having the time of our lives, we are also looking at my roommate's belongings. Besides the ugly flag, he's got pictures of half naked women in cowboy hats strung up all over the place, a corn snake in a small glass tank, and a strange white robe hanging in his closest that Louis and I dismiss right away as some freaky looking bathrobe or something.

After a few minutes, Louis turns down my stereo without my permission, and I yell at him.

"Shut up, Tabb," says Louis. "I got a very special surprise for you!"

"You're gonna get me laid?" I ask Louis, then stare down at my right hand, hoping to wish it a final good-bye.

"Better," replies Louis.

I tell my best friend that *nothing* is better than me getting laid. That having sex with a woman is the most important thing in my life, and that if I didn't do it soon, I'd implode.

"The Ramones are playing at the gym in an hour," explains Louis. "How's that?"

"How's that?" I yell. "How's that?"

I hug my best friend again and then tell him all about the last Ramones show I saw in New York at the Palladium a few months back, where the band rocked so hard that the people in the bleachers jumped up and down until the balcony we were on almost collapsed.

It had scared the shit out of Nick, who had taken me to see my favorite band in the world, but in the end, seeing the everlasting smile on my face, he knew it was well worth it.

And now they were playing here. Not five minutes from my dorm.

I looked up at my ceiling, trying to see the sky through it, and thanked the Almighty. Whoever she or he might be.

And then, with our leather jackets and ripped jeans, we made our way to our first Florida punk rock concert.

*

"One-two-twee-fo!" yells Dee Dee Ramone from the right side of the stage on the University of Florida's basketball court, and the Ramones plow into their thirty-six songs in seventy-two minutes set. And it's incredible.

Louis and I hop around, standing at first in front of lead singer Joey, then moving left toward Johnny. We jump up and down so much we find ourselves covered in sweat.

We have a good look around and everyone else is, as well. The opening band, the Chiclids, were a danceable new wave act, but the Ramones were the shit.

As they kick into "Pinhead" from *Today Your Love, Tomorrow the World*, our favorite song, some girl with a ripped Clash T-shirt bumps into both Louis and I. She's a few inches shorter than us, and has pretty green eyes and a nice nipple that is poking out next to Joe Strummer's head.

"Sorry," she says to us as she pogos away, while Louis and I just look at one another, then do the high-five thing.

As the set continues, I find myself bumping into the girl in the Clash shirt a few more times. Our eyes lock every once in a while, and we each dismiss it with a brief smile then more chants of "Hey Ho, Let's Go!"

Toward the end of the set, I tell Louis I need a quick break, then step back to look at what's around me.

Punk rockers. Hundreds of them. Some in leather jackets, some in torn T-shirts, and some with no tops on at all.

And it's wonderful.

Never, in Floriduh, have I ever felt so at home.

So on our walk back to my dorm that night, not driving my car because I wasn't allowed to bring it to school that first year, I tell Louis my feelings.

"It's like New York here," I say to my pal, who, I notice, also has new US pins to go with the new pleather jacket.

"Sort of," explains Louis, "there are certainly lots of cool folks about."

"And the non-cool ones?" I ask Louis, as we are still playing air guitar, while jumping all over the sidewalk imagining it to be our stage.

"You'll find those sorry ass suckers as well," he explains.

And a few minutes later, I do.

*

As I make my way into my new dorm room I see him.

My new and first roommate.

He's quite taller than me, and looks a lot more like Gomer Pyle or Barney Fife than the grizzly redneck biker I had imagined him to be.

His hair is cut shorter than mine, and he is dressed in a pair of faded blue jeans and a T-shirt that has some greek lettering on it.

"Hi," I say, making the awkward first move, as I make my way across my side of the small room into his. "I'm George!"

With that, I stick out my hand.

Gomer looks at my right hand likes he's never seen one before, then stares at my black leather jacket.

As his eyes slowly make their way up my body, they stop first at my nose for a few seconds before concentrating completely on my brown curly hair.

"A Jew?" he says, dumbfounded.

"Huh?" I ask.

"A biker Jew?" he asks again, more to himself then to me.

I withdraw my hand and say nothing.

"I get a motorcycle Jew for a roommate?" he asks, staring at the ceiling.

"If it makes you feel any better," I say, not liking this guy one bit, "I don't own a motorcycle. Do you?"

"Do I what?" he asks with a look of both confusion and hate in his eyes.

"Own a motorcycle?" I ask.

"No," he yells firmly, through his tightly clenched jaw.

"Well," I say, trying to make light of the bloodbath about to come, "I thought you did. I guess we were both wrong about each other, huh?"

The guy, realizing that it's now time to either shake hands or fight his new roommate for his well established territory, does the sensible thing.

He punches me in the nose.

Before I can swing back at the motherfucker, two guys run into the room and grab me from behind.

"I'm Doc," says one of the guys, who has huge forearms.

"And I'm Rich," says the other, who has nice smelling hair that's shoved up my nose.

"And we see you've met Jim," they both say in unison as they struggle to hold me back from cleaning the asshole's clock for good.

After a few seconds, they loosen their grip on me. But not completely.

"He just punched me in the nose!" I yell.

"Are you okay?" they both ask, rather caringly.

I turn around and look at the two gentlemen, who explain they live across the hall, while keeping one eye peeled on the scumbag they called Jim.

They seem like nice enough guys, both with white T-shirts, tucked into their stone washed jeans.

"I'm fine," I tell them.

"Good," says Doc. "We thought we'd see you before you got into your room."

"But we were late, huh?" continues Rich.

I just nod my head.

Suddenly Jim starts yelling at his two floormates to let me go so he can "kill the Jew."

"Ignore him," says Rich, who I notice has curly brown hair like mine, and a nose to match. "He hates us only because his father does. He doesn't know what he's doing."

"Yeah," adds Doc, whose light blonde hair is balding on his huge head that sits upon his huge body. "He drove his last two roomates crazy."

"Isn't this the freshman dorm?" I ask, confused.

Rich and Doc explain it is, and although they've been fine roommates for quite some time, Jim had a "nasty" habit of chasing those he shared his space with away.

"I can't understand why," I say sarcastically.

*

About a half hour later, I find myself wondering if I should bother unpacking the rest of my belongings at all.

As I sit there, on my crappy mattress, with a spring scratching my lower back, Jim opens his mouth up for the first time since Doc and Rich have left the room.

"Sorry about before," he mumbles, as he too sits on his bed, trying not to make eye contact with me.

I don't say anything.

"Sometimes," Jim explains, "I get a little over excited."

"A little over excited," I scream at the guy. "You fucking socked me in the nose!"

"I'm sorry," Jim whispers, as he cowers away from me and curls up into a little ball.

I look at him, and for the first time, see him how I suppose the others do.

More pathetic than me.

"Let's start over," I find myself saying. Then with my right hand again extended, "My name is George."

*

The next day, while Louis and I stand in line at registration, and then at financial aid, we talk about my new roommate.

"He sounds worse then the three dorks I share my pod with," says Louis.

"Three?" I ask him.

"Yeah," Louis explains. "I'm over in Johnson Towers. There are four of us sorry ass suckers in each pod. And a pod has two bedrooms and one bathroom."

I tell Louis he's got it pretty good. I share a room a Mayberry reject and share a bathroom with an entire half of a floor.

Louis laughs and then explains the Towers are not all they're cracked up to be. "The elevators take forever, so most days I find myself never leaving the floor."

I say nothing, but come to understand Louis's zero point zero grade average a bit better.

As the conversation turns to my roommate, Jim, once again, I tell Louis I've never seen such hatred since my days in Greenwich.

Or since my dad dropped me off. Yesterday.

Louis explains to me that we are in the middle of the state, which means that Gainesville draws all sorts of people from all walks of life.

As he's saying this, a well dressed kid walks up to the both of us and introduces himself.

"I'm Ken," he says to Louis and I. "And what might you gentlemen's names be?"

I tell Ken my name is George and the guy in the *fake* leather jacket likes to be called Louis.

"Hi George and Louis," Ken says, in a sort of eerie way, with a glazed look over his eyes. "Welcome to the University of Florida, and welcome to the beginnings of your new life!"

"Uh oh," says Louis, and starts to walk away from Ken and I.

"Where are you going?" I scream at Louis, embarrassed.

"I'm not doing *this* again," exclaims Louis, and with that, he disappears into a thick crowd of students.

I turn around and apologize to Ken.

"I'm sorry about my friend," I start, but Ken just puts his index finger to my lips and tells me it's all fine.

"Some people just don't like to make new friends," says Ken, in his button up and nicely ironed white shirt, wearing the kind of pants you would see on someone's father.

On his backpack I notice the letters TCCOC.

I've seen a couple of these backpacks already, but ignore them.

"Anyway," I say, "Louis is really nice and all but sometimes he just gets shy."

Ken explains that he knows *exactly* what I'm talking about, then asks if we can just be friends, even if it doesn't involve Louis.

The conversation, sounding more like a stupid soap opera, ends with me telling Ken that it would be nice to be friends, and then us exchanging phone numbers.

When I ask Louis later that day why he bolted from Ken and I, he tells me "There's lots to learn in life, Georgie Boy!"

*

"So, you're born that way?" asks Jim, as he lays on his bed while I sort through my record collection, trying to put them in alphabetical order. I'm having trouble deciding if bands that start with the word "the" should put it in the T section.

"What way?" I ask Jim, wondering if it's Ramones, or the Ramones.

"A Jew," he says.

I stop what I'm doing and look him in the face. I'm about to ask him if he's serious but can clearly see he is.

"We're all born who we are," I tell him. "So I guess I'm a Jew!"

"And I guess I'm a Christian," Jim exclaims happily and then laughs to himself.

I start to wonder if perhaps my new roommate may indeed have Down's Syndrome.

"Yup," is all I say, turning my attention back over to more important things. Like the word "the."

"So I'm born with the blood of Christ," Jim continues, "and you're born with the blood of Christ as well. On your hands!"

I ask him what the fuck he's talking about and he starts in on the whole Jews killed Jesus thing I used to hear in Connecticut.

"I wouldn't know," I tell the guy, not wanting to be drawn into this moron conversation. "I wasn't around back then."

"But it's true that the Jews killed Jesus," Jim explains, as he now happily bounces a pink rubber ball off the ceiling. "It's in the Bible."

I tell Jim there's lots of stuff in the Bible and to leave me alone. I'm busy.

An hour later I decide that the word "the" doesn't count.

Two hours later, I decide it does.

*

The next day as Jim and I dress to go to our first classes of the quarter, Jim watches as I put on my black Ramones T-shirt, ripped blue jeans, Converse All Courts, and black leather motorcycle jacket.

"Do you always walk around like that?" he asks, as I sprinkle some Brut 33 on my hard leather collar. I hate the feel of the stuff against my skin. It hurts. But Tommy Corn had told me that chicks dig it.

"Like what?" I ask him, as he tucks in his same T-shirt with the Greek lettering into another pair of stone washed jeans.

"Like a Mexican Jew," he says seriously.

Somehow able to read this guy's brain, which isn't much harder then reading "Go Dog Go," I explain to him the Ramones are not from south of the border, but from Queens, New York.

"Queens?" he asks.

"Yeah," I say, as I pick out my curly brown Jew-fro with the black afro pick my mom had given me as a birthday present a few months back. It had a black plastic fist with the words "black power" engraved across the top.

"That's so funny they name a section of Jew York City for the faggots," exclaims Jim, with excitement on his face like you'd see on a gorilla as you dangled a banana in front of his cage.

"Uh huh," I mumble, thoughts elsewhere, but mostly targeted on this huge zit that's growing on the left side of my nose, that's about to surface any day now.

"Anyway," says Jim, "have a great first day of college!"

I look at him and I think he means it. So I tell him to do the same.

*

I meet Louis in the student union where we quickly scarf down four scrambled eggs each and three pieces of bacon we've each charged to our meal card.

"Don't use up that thing too quickly," explains Louis, pointing at the yellow punch card I've now taken off my tray and am in the process of inserting back into my wallet.

"Why not?" I ask my pal in his owl framed glasses, which, I keep insisting, are not punk rock. He should buy the wrap-around kind of frames.

"If you don't blow all your money on chow with the food card," explains Louis, "you can always drink it later in beer."

In beer.

Holy shit!

Excitedly, I ask Louis about this and he tells me not to get my fishnets in a bunch. I tell him I've stopped wearing those since high school and we both have a good laugh.

"Seriously," Louis then explains, "you can gain more weight and have more fun with beer. So don't waste your meal vouchers on food!"

From that day on, I realize the value of nutrition, and its actions upon my growing brain, so I do the right thing and cut down to one meal a day.

Breakfast.

From then on it's beer for lunch at the Orange and Brew, a campus pub, then beer and chips for dinner at the campus Rathskeller.

And all is fine.

And hazy.

*

"Hi, Ken," I say to my new friend as Louis and I make our way into our first class, freshman English.

"Hi Louis and George," says Ken as he puts out his hand for us to shake. As we do, I hear Louis mumble, "Fuck, he's got our names down pat."

I ignore the sorry assed sucker, and ask Ken how things have been in the last twenty-four hours.

"Great, George," he says. "I've met plenty of new friends and am having a swell time."

"Cool," I say to Ken.

"Yes," says Ken, "it is cool, George."

We sit through class, and after the teacher begins to wrap things up by telling us about the hundreds of dollars of textbooks we are going to have to buy for the stupid class, Ken tells Louis and I he has a friend for us to meet.

Louis, quickly excusing himself, saying he's got a bad case of head lice, tells me he'll meet me in an hour at our next class. Freshman math.

"George," says Ken, as he introduces me to this beautiful blonde in a fuzzy pink sweater, "this is Kate. Kate, this is George."

As we shake hands, I feel the freshly applied moisturizer, and run my hand by my nose as soon as we've stopped touching. It smells nice.

"Kate is new here, too!" explains Ken.

I look at the vixen and think to myself that I wouldn't mind showing her around.

But before my brain can wander any further, I notice the letters TCCOC on her backpack. It matches Ken's.

"What's TCCOC?" I ask the both of them.

They just look at each other and politely laugh.

"Don't worry about it," says Kate, as she once again grabs my hand. "Let me walk you around the campus a bit and show you around. Then I'll take you to your next class."

Not thinking anything through because a beautiful blonde girl is touching me, I start to like college more and more.

*

Later that afternoon, after about my third or fourth class, as Louis and I walk towards the Rathskeller, two cute brunettes stop us in our tracks.

They are wearing really tight jeans and orange and blue T-shirts, the school's official colors, and they smell wonderful.

"Hi, George and Louis," they say, smiling at us.

We both look around to see what other George and Louis they could possibly be talking to.

Finally, I cough out the words, "Are you talking to us?"

"Of course we are," says Barbara, one of the brunettes. "Do you see any other Georges or Louises around?"

We both say nothing. We're tongue-tied.

"Are you liking college?" asks the other brown haired wonder, who tells us her name is also Barbara, but she is called Barbie so the two can separate each other.

I tell them we are, and my mind yells to me that I'm in love, and each girl is cuter than Bambi. Barbie. Whatever.

"Where are you off to?" asks Barbara number one.

Louis explains to them that we have some heavy drinking to do and they're not invited.

As the girls walk away, disappointed, I slug Louis as hard as I can on the arm in his *fake* leather jacket.

"What the fuck?" I scream.

"Look at their backpacks, George," Louis says and I do.

I see those letters TCCOC printed on them.

"You know what that means?" asks Louis.

I tell him I don't.

So he explains it to me over lunch.

Of beer and french fries, of course.

*

"How was your day, Jew Boy?" asks Jim as I stumble into our stuffy abode, trying to balance all the heavy textbooks I've just purchased. The total for these things is well over five hundred bucks.

"Until I had to stand in line at the student bookstore," I say. "It was fine."

"Why are *you* buying books?" asks Jim. "Don't you Jews know everything already?"

I tell him that while we do, sometimes we like to read about the old country.

"What old country?" he asks. "Jew land?"

I tell him about Transylvania, and how we have all descended upon the rest of the world from there. I explain that while our ancestors may have dabbled in imbibing blood, we've come a long way since then and now find that same nutrition in tomato juice.

As I'm telling him his, his jaw is around his ankles, and I think he's buying every word.

"Yeah," I continue, "Translyvania was a beautiful country, with lush green landscapes and blood cherries that grew on the vine."

"What happened to it?" asks Jim, dumbfounded.

"Alas," I explain, "it sunk into the ocean with Atlantis over ten thousand years ago. The few survivors who managed to swim away were picked up by alien spaceships and taken to Vulcan, where their culture and ours have now become one."

At this point, Jim finally realizes I'm pulling this stuff out of my ass as I go along and laughs.

And it's a nice laugh. An honest one.

"You're so full of shit," he tells me, with a broad smile across his face.

Trying to separate my fingers, I hold up my hand and tell him "Live long and prosper."

*

The next day, while sitting in freshman English with Ken and Kate, I notice Louis is strangely absent. He didn't show up to breakfast, and when I called him at his pod in Johnson Towers, he told me he doesn't feel like going out today.

Whatever.

"So, how are things?" asks Ken, with that still glazed over and faraway look in his eyes.

"Yeah?" asks Kate. I look into her eyes and see the same look. The best I can describe it is like those looks those dead people give you in movies right before they eat your living flesh. It's a look that says nothing, means nothing, and to tell you the truth, sort of gives me the creeps.

"Listen guys," I say to my new living dead pals, "I asked Louis about those letters on your backpacks and he's told me what they stand for."

"The Crossroads Church of Christ," says Ken calmly. Kate nods her head.

"Well," I start, "while I like to respect everyone's views, and I do, I just think—"

I'm cut off by another fellow with the letters TCCOC on his backpack.

He's huge, standing well over six feet, and has the nicest blue eyes I've ever seen.

On a man.

He's hovering over all of us and finally asks to be introduced to me.

"Blake," says Ken, "this is George. George this is Blake. And we all know Kate."

Everyone politely laughs, and after class, Blake asks me if I've got plans before my next science class that's at least two hours away.

Wondering how the hell he knows what my schedule is, I tell him it's fine if we hang out. As long as it's at the Orange and Brew, and we can drink beer.

Blake tells me that's totally cool with him.

*

As we sit in the dimly lit pub, sharing a huge pitcher of Black Label beer, Blake tells me more about his "group" at my prodding.

"We're just like you and everyone else," explains Blake, "except we've let Jesus Christ into our souls."

"How does he get in," I ask, "with the keys you leave under the flower pot or a credit card and paperclip? I hear that works well."

Blake laughs, and I must admit, it's a nice laugh.

"No, silly," explains Blake, "Jesus enters your heart because you choose to let him in."

I think about that for few seconds and decide it's not for me. One person in me is enough already, and I really hate roommates, especially the one I have now.

"You won't even know he's there," explains Blake, somehow reading my thoughts.

"Well," I say, "if I don't, then what good is he?"

Blake explains to me that Jesus can help steer me in the right directions in life and will forgive me for all of my sins.

I tell him I don't sin, whatever that is.

"Do you masturbate?" asks Blake, loud enough for only me to hear it.

It jolts me.

"Umm," I stammer.

"Come on, George," says Blake, with his kind blue eyes, "do you play with yourself?"

"A lot," I confess.

"And how do you feel about that?" Blake asks.

Not knowing why I'm even bothering with this conversation, I find myself telling Blake that sometimes I do it six times in twenty-four hours. And that's on a slow day.

"Did you know Jesus considers that a sin?" he then asks.

"Huh?" I say.

"A sin. Something bad," explains Blake.

I ask him why it's bad, I mean, besides from the self injury I keep inflicting upon myself. Sometimes I rub it until it bleeds. Then, sometimes more.

"Because Jesus says so" is Blake's answer.

"Why should I take his word for it?" I ask Blake.

He just laughs and tells me I've got a lot to learn.

I feel like he's acting like Louis, excuse myself, and bolt.

*

That night, I ask Jim about the Crossroads Church of Christ.

"What the fuck are you messing with them for?" he asks. Then, a light bulb goes off over his head.

"You're a Jew!" he exclaims.

"Duh," I say.

"No," explains Jim, "they *love* Jews."

When I ask him what the fuck he's talking about he tells me he's late for a meeting.

He grabs that white hooded robe thing he's got hanging in his closet and runs out the door without even saying good-bye. I'd feel hurt if I wasn't so confused.

So I walk across the hall to Doc and Rich, and knock on their door.

"One second," screams Rich, and when he finally does open the door, I see Doc zipping up his jeans.

"We're on our way to a party," explains Rich, "and we were just changing."

"Okay," I say. "Anyway, what do you guys know about the Crossroads Church of Christ?"

"They're fine folks," laughs Doc, as he shaves in his dorm sink, and I find myself jealous because I can't grow hair on my face.

"No, really?" I ask.

Rich tells me they are a Christian cult and to stay as far away from them as possible. When I ask him why, he tells me he has no time to explain right now, and with that, he and Doc are out the door. Wearing matching purple shirts for some reason.

*

"Listen, Ken," I say to my new friend in class the next morning, after having breakfast with Louis but before losing him on the way to class, "I know you guys are all into Jesus and all, and that's cool, but I just am not."

"That's fine," says Kate. "We understand nonbelievers."

I try to explain to them that's it's not a case of not believing, it's rather a case of having other things to worry about at the time.

"But Jesus can help you with everything," says Blake, sitting behind us with a hot babe named Monica, who also wears the official Crossroads Church of Christ backpack.

Monica's eyes are brown and pretty, but for some reason they don't have that distant look in them.

And she smells heavenly.

"Yes," says Monica, as I watch awe in the way her lovely full red lips move against her pale white skin "Jesus Saves. Us all."

After class, Ken asks if we can all meet up later to discuss the whole Jesus thing, and figuring that Louis has abandoned me, tell them "why not."

It's arranged that around six that evening, Blake and Ken, along with Kate and, sigh, Monica, will come to my dorm room to do something called a "Bible study."

While I'm not thrilled at the aspect of having more moron conversations, I do want to see Monica in my room, where I can show off all my cool Ramones albums and those rare Sex Pistols singles I hardly show to anyone.

And so, the date is set in stone.

*

Later that afternoon, after drinking way too much beer with Louis at the Rathskeller and laughing about the fact I've yet to crack open a book, I ask Louis if he'd like to join me in my dorm for a "Bible study," whatever that was.

Louis, who's not only not cracked open a book, but hasn't even purchased one, tells me he'll pass. He says he and his roomates are playing this wicked game of D&D, and he's about to be promoted to dungeon master.

So I return to Graham Hall, alone.

When I get to my dorm's lobby, I see Ken, Blake, Monica, Kate, and a new face who is introduced to me as Jill, Ken's girlfriend.

I think about the fact that Ken has a girlfriend and realize that maybe Jesus can help me get one, too.

As we make our way to my room in the basement, the other guys on my floor stare at me in shock as I walk with my new friends into my room.

Then they all giggle behind my back, but no one says anything aloud.

Once we all get into my tiny prison cell, everyone asks where to sit and I say "wherever."

So Blake sits at my desk, while Ken and Jill sit on Jim's bed.

And Monica, sweet Monica, sits next to me.

"Are you ready, George?" asks Ken.

"Ready for what?" I ask.

"To learn about the true path," says Ken.

As I stare at Monica's tightly wrapped legs in her skintight blue jeans, I follow the stitching on the sides all the way up to her firm and nicely rounded ass. I also take in her wonderful aroma.

"Path, yeah, whatever," I say.

Ken takes out a bunch of bibles from his TCCOC backpack and gives us each a copy. Then he tells us to open it to a certain page and find a certain paragraph.

While I'm doing this, I can't help but peek over at Monica, who, for some reason, turns to the wrong page but says nothing.

"Jesus tells us," Ken begins, "that all our sins—"

Suddenly my dorm door flies open, and it's Jim.

My Mayberry roommate.

"Jim," I say, "this is Monica and Blake and Ken and Jill!"

"NIGGERS!" yells Jim, at the top of his lungs.

"Huh?" I say.

"Niggers!" yells Jim again. "There are niggers on my bed."

I look over at Ken and Jill, who look shocked.

"It's bad enough I have to sleep next to a Jew," Jim screams, going into a hysterical episode, "but niggers? On my bed? I'm going to have to burn the sheets!"

"Maybe we should excuse ourselves," mumbles Blake.

"You let Bible-thumping niggers in here?" Jim screams. He then looks at Blake and Monica.

"What's your problem?" he yells. "Are you homos?"

"I'm French," says Blake.

"Oh, great," yells Jim, "that's even worse. All of you, out of my room, now!"

At a loss for something, anything, to say, I watch as my new friends pack up their belongings and leave. We all promise to meet up in the morning during second block.

*

Later that night, while Jim washes his sheets next door in the dorm's laundry room, I ask him just what exactly his problem is.

"No problem," explains Jim. "Niggers have germs that kill white people, so I'm killing those germs."

When I ask him what kind of germs, he tells me he doesn't know, but his father does.

"What else does your father know?" I ask him, curious.

"He knows about all the mutt and mud races," Jim explains.

Prodding him a little further, I ask Jim about his father.

"What about him?" Jim asks.

So I ask him what he does for work, how he lives his life, all that sort of stuff.

I think the next morning, while I'm sharing my eggs with Louis at breakfast because he's already blown his meal ticket for the day, I'm still in shock.

*

"His father is an imperial wizard for the Ku Klux Klan?" asks Louis, as bits of egg fly about the cafeteria.

"I think they call it Knights in White Satin or something," I try to explain to Louis.

"Tabb," seethes Louis, "you sorry ass sucker, your roomates' father will kill you if he ever sees you!"

I ask Louis more about this Ku Klux Klan thing, or "KKK" as he likes to refer to them, and Louis tells me all about it.

Having lived his entire life in the South, Louis explains to me he's very familiar with "their sort." He says they are a racial hatred group who used to hang black people from trees and burn crosses on their lawns, but now have moved into burning down people's churches. And temples.

"They don't like Jews, either?" I ask.

"If you're not white," says Louis, "you're not right."

I tell Louis that that's a fucked up way of looking at things and he tells me to tell him about it. He then tells me this story of about how, when he was about five, he and his Italian family found a burning cross on their lawn in Tallahassee.

"But you're not black!" I say to Louis.

"Didn't matter," explains Louis, now a bit more calm. "Even though we were Italian, my father hired a few black guys to work at his store. That was enough for them."

"So if you even associate with black people they hate you?" I ask.

"There's only one thing they hate more than Negroes and 'nigger lovers' as they call them," Louis says.

*

"Yup," says Jim, "we hate Jews worse than anyone."

As I ask him why that afternoon in my dorm, where we've both decided that classes just weren't for us that day, Jim explains.

"Jews own everything. They own all the money in the world, and, unlike good Christians, don't keep their race pure," Jim says.

When I tell Jim I've got no money and don't own a damn thing except my leather jacket, he points out my father.

"He's a rich kike from up north," says Jim. "Right?"

I tell him he is, but that I don't see any of that money. Not one dime.

"Doesn't matter," explains the skinny kid in the same T-shirt with the Greek letters. "Jews keep the money all to themselves and don't share it with anyone."

I think about what Jim has just said and it does sort of ring true. My father has never given me a dime. But then I remember my mother, and how generous she and Nick are.

"Bullshit," I finally say, "you guys are just trying to find someone to hate!"

"No," says Jim, calmly, "we already have. And it's you. The Bible tells us so. You're going to hell."

*

That night I have the scariest dreams I've had since I was little. I dream that I'm engulfed in flames while everyone around me pretends I'm not there screaming in agony. They just walk past me on the University of Florida campus, carrying their books, and talking amongst themselves about how Jesus has taught them "the way."

I see Louis there as well, and it seems he can see me. He tells me I'm a sorry ass sucker, then suddenly grows a beard.

Before I know it, he's screaming in pain as nails are being pounded into each of his hands, and then one through both feet.

As I step back to look at him, I see he's been nailed to a giant flaming phallus, which looks exactly like mine.

I try to put the flames out by rubbing my own penis, but the more I do so, the more Louis screams in pain.

Finally, unable to bear the screaming anymore, I scream louder.

Loud enough to wake me from that horrible dream.

*

"I think I need your help," I say to Blake the next morning as we sit together over breakfast. I'd called him at the number he gave me, and he beat me to the student union with less than five minutes notice.

"What's up?" asks Blake, as he stares at me with those blank but pretty blue eyes.

"I'm afraid I'm going to Hell," I tell him in all seriousness.

"Why?" he asks.

I tell him about the dream. The horrible dream.

"Jesus can help you," Blake says, and with that, smiles. It's one that says "trust me."

So I do.

"While masturbation is only one sin, there are plenty you don't know about," explains Blake. "Why not come to our barbeque tonight?"

I ask him about the cookout and he tells me lots of fine folks from the church are going to be there, as well as some possible newcomers, like myself.

I take him up on his offer, and walk around campus the rest of that day looking forward to some kind of salvation.

Guilt about fights with my father, my mom leaving me, and those dirty thoughts of sex dance around in my brain.

I hope like hell I can get rid of them. Before it's too late.

*

That evening, as I'm introduced to many of Blake's and Ken's friends in the Crossroads Church of Christ at some barbeque, where the smell of freshly grilled hamburgers excite my nose, I sort of feel at home.

Everyone is very kind to me, and they all seem to ask sincere questions.

"Was your childhood bad?" asks this one cute girl, Dawn.

"Was it good is the better question," I tell her.

She explains to me that her upbringing was horrible. That her father had molested her, as well as her brother. And when she got pregnant at fourteen, she was sent away and never returned home.

"I'm sorry," I say, speechless.

"Don't be," says Dawn, as a warm smile makes its way across her face, "I've found Jesus, and he loves me for who I am!"

I hear similar stories all that evening, some involving drugs, and others, alcohol. But rape seems to be the popular theme.

At the end of the night I feel like I've gotten to know these people pretty darn well, and for all they've been through, they certainly are still very nice. Nice to the point where I want in.

*

The next day, while laying out in the warm Florida sun with both our leather jackets on, real and *fake*, I tell Louis I'm thinking about joining the Crossroads Church of Christ.

When he asks why, I tell him that I've really made some good friends, and even, today, on campus, about ten people who I hardly remembered meeting last night, remembered my name and gave me a friendly hello.

"That's how they work," explains Louis.

"Who works," I ask.

"Religious cults," says Louis. "First they sucker you in, then make you feel bad for all the stuff you've done, then make you sign up!"

"Then what happens?" I ask my pal.

"Then you find yourself giving flowers out at the airport, digging ditches on a farm in China, or worse, trying to convert others into your loser lifestyle."

Finally, dropping all pretenses, I tell Louis what's really on my mind.

"I don't want to go to Hell," I say to him.

"Hell is here on Earth," explains Louis, "as well as Heaven. It's all how you look at things."

I look over at him laying on the soft grass in his *fake* leather jacket and start to wonder if I haven't been missing something with this guy over the last couple of years.

*

The rest of that week continues on with my crash course in Christianity. From Blake and Ken I learn about other awful things I've done and need to be forgiven for, and from Jill and Kate, that while they too have sexual urges, they now understand they must control them until marriage.

But I think the person I most learn from is Monica.

She asks me how I feel about everything, and when I tell her, she and her red pouty lips just smile. Her pale skin glows with a freshness I've rarely seen, and while everyone else tells me that Jesus will solve my problems, Monica doesn't give me that kind of answer at all.

In fact, she tells me it's up to *me* to solve my problems.

While I find this strange, coming from a girl with a back-pack that has the letters TCCOC on it, I do listen to her.

And consider deeply what she has to say.

*

So there I am, sitting on this hardwood bench bench with my testicles in a twist, sweating to the point where it's hard to see the hippie looking preacher guy on the stage a few rows in front of me.

On stage with him are Blake, Ken, Jill, and Kate. Barbara and Barbie are off to the side.

"So," continues the priest, pastor, master-of-puppets, or whatever you want to call him, "tonight we welcome into our flock a Jew!"

Everyone claps and looks at me.

And I look back at them.

Feeling wanted.

And it's a nice feeling.

One I'm not often used too.

"Tonight," Manson Christ continues, "we are welcoming one of the Lord's killers. One with blood on his hands, but a beating passion in his heart!"

Everyone claps as I begin to let the preacher's words sink in.

"We have with us tonight," he yells, "a sinner. Of the worst kind!"

That's when the cheering begins.

"Tonight he will meet Jesus Christ," he continues, "and be cleansed of his filthy filthy sins."

I start to not like this so much.

"He's come to us a dirty Jew, having been abused by his father and by the horrible world of drugs," Jesus Mansion continues, "and a shameless self-fornicator of the worst kind! But tonight, we will free him of all the awful sins he has committed against us and welcome him into our arms as well of those of Jesus."

Sins against them? Christ killer?

I really start to think hard about what I'd said to Jim a few days earlier. I *really* wasn't around when Jesus got strung up, and I didn't know if the Bible told the truth, anyway.

And about the sins against them? What did I ever do to Ken, Blake, Jill, or Kate?

All I offered them was a pair of ears and an openness in my heart.

And what'd they do with that? They told this maniac preacher about my innermost feelings.

But worse, it began to dawn on my slow mind that it wasn't "George" they were trying to help, but "A Jew."

Or "save," as they put it.

From Hell.

A place where the devil lived and where I would go for all the bad things I'd done like trying to make peace with my father. Trying to protect my younger brothers from whatever the world could throw at them. Finding the innocence in beauty in all of God's creatures, and loving them for that.

And I was still going to go to Hell because of some guy I never met? Some hippie two thousand years dead, who talked to these freaks from beyond the grave?

Right.

"Fuck you," I say as I stand up that hot spring day in Florida. "Fuck you and all this bullshit!"

And with that, I walk out of that stinking church, forever.

*

A few minutes later, while steaming mad, I bump into Monica as I stomp my way back toward my dorm.

"It went that well, huh?" she says, as she grabs my chin and forces me to look into her warm brown eyes.

I notice once again, even through my fury, that she doesn't have that lost look.

"Where were you?" I scream at her, lashing out at the world.

"Letting you find yourself," she explains. "Letting your soul be free."

I'm about to ask her what the fuck she's talking about, but the next second, she's gone.

And all that's left is her angelic aroma.

ANIMAL FARM

SO THERE I AM, in my black leather jacket, listening to the other guys in my fraternity, Sigma Nu, explaining why I should once again try and talk to the blonde Tri Delt.

"She's really hot, George," explains Todd, who has somehow taken a liking to me and is the only other Jewish member of the frat.

"But she's mean and—" I start.

"Plus," continues Todd, "she's a Tri Delt. They're our sister sorority. If you ever want to score any pussy in your life, this is your best chance."

I look at Todd, then at the blonde who had just told me to fuck off.

Although her beautiful blonde hair and perfect Barbie doll body make my crotch ache, that neon sign in her eyes flashing Vacancy sort of puts me off.

"Maybe I'll meet someone else," I suggest to Todd and his Sigma Nu golfing shirt, as he pumps the keg and then pours us more beers that fateful night at the "mixer," as someone had called it.

"You are going to walk over to her like a true Sigma Nu," states Todd, "and work on getting into her pants."

"But she's wearing a skirt," I protest.

Todd just gives me that look.

The same one he had given me a week earlier. When he swung a baseball bat at my head.

And the same look that Wally, another fraternity brother, had given me. When he swung a nine iron at my head.

So I walk over to her once again.

"Hi," I say, sticking out my hand for her to shake. "Once again, my name is George and I'm a pledge here at Sigma Nu."

"Fuck off, Jew," she says, as she dismisses me with the symbolic flick of her fingers then goes about talking to her friends.

I walk away, frustrated and feeling stupid for being in this situation in the first place. If I hadn't tried to join a fraternity like my father wanted me too, none of this would be happening.

But now, here, at this stupid apartment complex at the University of Florida, I was being torn to pieces by Ilsa, She-Wolf of the SS.

"What the fuck are you doing?" gargles Wally, as he stands next to Todd in his Hawaiian shirt and Bermuda shorts, complete with penny loafers, silly hat, and sunglasses, drinking as fast as he can from the tap on the keg. "Get back over there and score some pussy. Or you're out."

I think about that for a second and wonder if being out is such a bad thing. I was really starting to not like these people, and it was certainly not turning out to be like the movie I so worshiped, *Animal House*.

Stirring me from thoughts comes Chris, an ex-brother, who is now an active Marine. He stands about six feet four, weighs more than Superman, and has the muscles and self-esteem to match.

"What's wrong, buddy?" he asks me as he puts his giant arm around my shoulders. He's in town for this party, he's told me, then he's back off to some base in Germany or something where he's employed as a drill sergeant.

I tell Chris about the Tri Delta's rejection, then about how Todd and Wally are riding my ass about it.

"Well then," he says in his macho superhero voice, as he stands next to me in full military dress, "let's just go have a talk with this little bunny!"

So, me and this tall Marine walk up to the Tri Delt, who is now busy talking to some of her "sisters." As we approach, they all stop talking and stare at us. Blankly.

I wonder if just perhaps they are members of the Crossroads Church of Christ or some other campus cult.

"What do you want?" screams the blonde. "I told you to go away!"

I try explaining to her that my brothers in Sigma Nu would really like it if she would just talk to me for a couple of minutes, as Chris, silently nods his head.

What comes out of her mouth next is so offensive and incredible that a few minutes later, Chris and I find ourselves not only on the run from my brothers at Sigma Nu, and all the Tri Deltas, but from the Gainesville Police Department as well.

But let me back up a bit.

*

After my first week of college, and my whole clash with a Christian cult that carefully tried to crucify me, I found myself not trusting a whole lot of human beings.

Sure, I'd met some mighty fine folks on the campus of the University of Florida, but the only guy I could trust was my high school friend, Louis.

Louis, who wore the black owl framed glasses and never left his dorm room.

Louis, who probably attended three classes with me that first week of school before deciding he'd had enough, and would try and let his zero point zero grade point average slip even lower.

But I wasn't attending college for that.

I was there to get drunk, learn a few things about women, I hoped, and finally get laid before it would be too late and I'd die of sperm backup.

My Ku Klux Klan roommate, Jim, explained to me one morning before my first class that he had hoped for the same thing.

"To score less than a zero point zero GPA?" I ask him, as he puts on his underwear, followed by his stonewashed jeans, and that same T-shirt with the greek lettering I found out to be the initials for Kappa Alpha, the "white" fraternity on campus.

By "white" I mean, well, white. Kappa Alpha is a fraternity that has it's roots dug deeply in the South, and all those guys in that good ol' boys' club rode around in pickup trucks yelling "The South Will Rise Again," like the Civil War hadn't ended over a hundred years earlier.

Whatever.

"Not that," explains Jim, about Louis's grades, or lack of them. "About getting laid. Isn't that why we're all here?"

I look at Gomer Pyle as he finishes getting dressed and realize we both have a lot more in common than just hate.

"I suppose it is," I tell him, "I feel like if I don't lose my virginity, I'll never be a man."

Jim nods his head in agreement, plucks out a few nose hairs with his fingers, then makes his way through my side of the room to the door.

"Listen, Jew," he says, "for what it's worth, I do hope you find some pussy this quarter."

With that he walks out of the room. Leaving me angry, frustrated, and surprisingly optimistic about the human race.

Of course, I lose that mood an hour later during my first class.

Bowling.

*

I must admit it wasn't my brilliant idea to take a bowling class at eight in the morning.

It was Louis's. He said we could be as drunk as we wanted to be, and as long as we showed up and knocked down a few pins a couple of times a week, we'd pass the course.

How wrong he was.

And I think he realized this, because after the first week of trying to line up those heavy black balls with those thin white pins in the student union, Louis had stopped showing up.

"Are you guys reading for today's lesson," asks Amy, our "instructor", as she stands on the bowling court in her cowboy boots, western style, button up shirt, and wavy brown hair covered by her cowboy hat.

We all sort of nod our heads, trying to shake away the morning's fog.

"Good," continues Amy, "today we are going to learn about picking up spares."

I look around at my other classmates, who probably thought this would be an easy PE credit as well, and realize the only thing any of us is going to pick up is a cold. We're all drunk or hungover, and it was clear our brains hurt.

Each of us, in some way, was holding our heads.

"A little too much partying?" asks Amy, as she picks up a bowling ball and holds it above her head, showing off a cute little belly button. "That's what you get your first quarter of college!"

With that she throws the ball as hard as she can down the wooden lane and as the ball hits the pins, it reverberates so loud in our brains we all scream in agony.

"Good morning," Amy says to us, "and welcome to the first day of the rest of your lives."

*

"Dad," I say to my father on our dorm phone after the first couple of weeks of college, "guess what?"

"I don't have time for this," my father yells at me, then hangs up the phone.

I call him back and explain to him that I've decided to pledge a fraternity.

"A what?" he screams so loudly I can hear our dogs start barking in the background.

I explain to him it's called Sigma Nu, and they are really nice guys.

"Are they Jews?" he asks.

I'm confused. When did my father ever care about Jews before?

"Uh," I say, "a couple of them."

"Well if you're going to join a frat," my father explains, "it had better be a Jewish one!"

When I ask him why, he explains to me that it's not the friendships and connections I make now that mean anything, it's what others can do for you in the future because they owe you favors.

Not knowing what the hell my father is ranting about, I thank him for his advice and hang up the phone.

"He wants you to be with your kind, huh?" says Jim, who has obviously been listening to this whole conversation although he looked like he was reading a text book. With an issue of Playboy hidden inside.

"Yeah," I say to Jim, "go figure."

"It makes sense," explains Jim, as he puts down the text-book on his bed, as a photo of a huge boobie pokes its way out. "People like their own kind."

I explain to Jim that my father never fucking cared about "his own kind" before, and that he is completely off his rocker.

"It's a money thing," explains Jim, "and with Jews, that's everything."

I tell him he doesn't know what he's talking about and leave the room, slamming the door behind me.

The truth was, I was pissed because some of what Jim said rang true.

*

When I first found Sigma Nu during rush week, I immediately knew it was the brotherhood for me. Besides having a house off campus, because they'd burnt theirs down the year before, the guys honestly didn't seem to give a shit if I wore a leather jacket and Ramones T-shirt or not, and the fact that I was a Jew didn't even play into things.

Or so I thought.

When Louis and I entered their rundown shack of a house on the outskirts of the student ghetto that first night, I knew we had found home.

There, in front of us, stood a guy with blondish brown hair, who introduced himself as Joe.

"Don't look behind me," he says, trying to block our view of some movement going on near his legs.

Of course we do and see this blonde girl, with her pants pulled down around her ankles, peeing in a patch of grass.

We could see the hair around her vagina and everything.

"You didn't look?" asks Joe with a smile on his face as Louis and I look at one another, amazed.

"Naw," we say.

"Good," laughs Joe, and with that, introduces us to the girl who had been squatting behind him a few seconds earlier "Guys this is Kelly. Kelly, this is . . ."

"I'm George and this is my friend, Louis," I say, sticking out my hand, "and we're damn glad to meet you!"

"*Animal House*?" asks Joe.

I nod my head and he laughs, then tells me I'm going to love it here.

*

That night Louis and I get so drunk we find ourselves pissing on the house's trashy lawn as well. The lines for the bathroom are way too long, and as we find ourselves peeing on broken garden gnomes and empty cans of Budweiser, not to mention scattered female underwear, we feel good.

"This place is just like the movie," I say to Louis as I zip up my jeans, not noticing I hadn't finished peeing yet, and therefore winding up with a huge urine stain that ends up being a bitch to cover with my Ramones T-shirt. I have to stretch the thing at least two inches longer, which almost ruins it.

"Tell me about it," says Louis. "These guys don't seem to care about anything!"

As Louis says that, a trophy of some sort breaks through the glass of a third story window, and lands directly in front of us. We pick it up and and see a sturdy block mantle with a brass vagina on top of it. The words "World's Best Pussy Eater" are inscribed in stone.

To top things off, buying a soda from the Sigma Nu's Coca-Cola machine on their porch and getting a can of Bud only helps seal the deal.

*

"Today," explains Amy, the morning after the wild Sigma Nu party, "we are going to learn about pin height and weight. And about bowling etiquette."

"What the fuck?" I mouth, and suddenly realize Amy sees me.

"What, George?" demands Amy. "What are you thinking?"

"Nothing," I tell my teacher in her leopard skin cowboy hat, with snakeskin boots on her feet today.

"Some of you think bowling is not important," says Amy, staring me directly in the eyes, "but some of you know different."

Amy then explains to us that bowling goes all the way back through history to the times of prehistoric man. That they used to roll rocks against slabs of stone, trying to knock over other stones. And that this, somehow, became a hunting method that would evolve later into bows and arrows, and, eventually, guns.

Lots of students take notes, but I sit back and laugh.

I start to like this Amy cowgirl.

And to prove it, when it's my turn to bowl, I roll a perfect strike.

It's just too bad the ball hits the pins two lanes over.

*

The night arrives that Louis and I have both been waiting for. The one where they tell us if we have made it to pledge status or not.

We both really want to be in Sigma Nu, so we talk about it during that day at the Rathskeller over a pitcher of Black Label.

"Georgie boy, I can't wait until we're pledges, then brothers," Louis says excitedly.

Always looking on the bright side of life, I ask Louis about what happens if they don't want us.

"They do," he says.

"Well what if they only want one of us?" I then ask.

Louis, with a look of confidence I've never seen in his eyes before, tells me that they want the both of us and that's that.

"Besides," he says, "we're the only two pledges, besides that other George guy."

The other George guy shares my name but nothing else. He's much taller than I am, has bright red hair, and walks and talks with the confidence of someone who's had sex.

Many times.

"Well, yeah," I say. "I suppose they'll want him, too."

*

But they don't.

Want Louis, that is.

We find out that night as we sit in the "living room" of the Sigma Nu house. On milk crates. It seems someone had set the furniture on fire the night before, and now, the place had the strong stench of burnt wood.

"It's not that we don't like you, Louis," explains Joe, as nicely as he can. "It's just that we don't see you as Sigma Nu material."

When I ask why, Wally just says "zero point zero."

"But this quarter I'm going to try harder," Louis protests.

I watch as everyone rolls their eyes and can't help but feel the same way. Louis already had stopped showing up for classes, and it was explained very clearly to us when we asked to pledge that the house had to have a C grade point average or better.

"Come on," I say to the guys, as they drink beers and don't seem to take this whole situation to seriously. "Louis is my best friend, and without him, well, I don't wanna join!"

Everyone gets quiet and looks at me.

"Is that really what you want?" asks Joe, with a very serious look in his eyes.

Before I can answer, Louis speaks up.

"Guys," he says, in his owl framed glasses and *fake* leather jacket, "I really don't want to be in a frat anyway."

We all look at him. Stunned.

"In reality," lies Louis, "I just wanted to see here if my sorry-ass sucker friend, George, would really go through with this."

Everyone laughs, and Louis further breaks the ice by saying even though he's not going to be a member of "their" fraternity, he is gonna stop by and check up on me. To make sure they're taking care of my urgent pussy situation, or UPS, as he calls it.

I look at my friend and feel tears well up in my eyes.

So I pretend to be sick from the beer, run to the bathroom, and make all sorts of vomiting noises.

When I exit, Louis is standing there with two full cans of Budweiser in his hands.

"Drink another," says Louis. "It's the hair of the dog thing, you know?"

But I know he knew I was faking it.

*

"So they took in a Jew," screams Jim, the next night, as I put on a Ramones album and blast it louder than Lynyrd Skynrd's "Freebird" he's got blaring from his Archer Stereo System.

"Yeah," I scream back to Jim, who's playing air guitar, only hitting all the wrong notes.

Eventually we both turn down our stereos, and Jim tries to talk to me. Seriously.

"You know," he starts out, "it's not all fun and games."

I tell Jim I know that. That it's also drinking and pussy.

"No," explains Jim, "that's not what I mean. They're going to want something serious from you."

Laughing, I ask him what they could ever want from me.

"I don't know," says Jim, honestly. "It could be something as little as telling you not to wear your leather jacket anymore."

"That's little?" I ask.

We have a good laugh before blasting our stereos at one another once more.

If only I'd really listened to him that night.

*

A few weeks later I find myself at bowling class. It's 8:15 AM and I'm late.

"Why are you so punctual?" asks Amy, surprisingly wearing no cowboy hat, and letting her brown hair beautifully reflect the florescent lights above.

"The Sigma Nu guys had me pushing around an egg with my nose then reading our creed over and over again," I tell her honestly.

"Why?" asks Amy. The simplest question in the world I find myself unable to answer.

"I don't know," I finally utter.

She just looks at me, then explains to the class that today we have to make at least three spares to pass this sort of pop-quiz.

Of course, I fail miserably.

*

"George," yells Joe for the third time, finally getting my attention.

We are sitting in his trailer, which is parked on Sigma Nu's lawn. It's his "pad," and we're watching porno movies with a couple of girls. Joe is showing them on his new Super Eight projector and I'm in awe.

Of the porn that is.

Until then, I'd never seen an X-rated movie.

Now, on screen, in front of me, I see hairy women and men do things I couldn't have imagined in my wildest of dreams.

There are men on top of women.

Women on top of men.

Men inside of women.

And lots and lots of goo.

It has me so turned on it must be making me deaf.

"So what do you think, George?" asks Joe, for the fourth time.

I try and tell him but find my tongue stiff.

"Thunderfawl" is all I can spit out.

The girls in the trailer laugh, then politely ask me if they can be alone with Joe.

"But George here is my little brother," Joe and his thick mustache explain. "What you have to say to me you can also say to him."

"It's not what we want to say," giggles one of the girls.

"Yeah," breathes the other.

"Will you ladies excuse us for a second?" says Joe, and then walks me out of his trailer.

"You do know what's going on, don't you?" asks Joe, with a real look of concern on his face as we stand in the yard of Sigma Nu.

"Yeth," I say, lying.

"No you don't, do you?" asks Joe.

I just stare at the ground and say nothing.

"Look, George," he explains, "I'm really glad you picked me as your big brother, and by doing so, I want to give you the greatest gift anyone could give someone else."

"Pussthy?" I ask.

Now it's Joe's turn to look at the ground.

"No," says Joe. "Friendship."

I wonder what the fuck I want with friendship. I have enough of that, and now it's time to, as Sally had called it, "take on a lover."

"You're not ready for anything else yet," explains Joe, still looking at the ground.

I try to get up the energy to protest, but for some reason, just can't.

While I'll admit to myself I'm totally turned on by what I've seen just now on Joe's refrigerator, where the projector was aimed, I have no idea how to execute those thoughts in reality.

And Joe somehow knows this.

"Look," says Joe, "you should go back in the house with the other guys and forget that what's about to happen happened."

I nod my head, sort of understanding him, but not really, and do as he says.

A few minutes later, from outside the kitchen window, I hear the girl's voices moaning.

And those familiar feelings of rage and abandonment swell inside my brain.

*

"How's the whole frat thing going?" asks Louis, later that quarter.

I've run into him at the student union, where he's busy setting the high score on a sit-down version of Space Invaders.

"You know," I say, trying not to be specific.

"That good, huh?" says Louis, without lifting his eyes from the aliens dropping bombs on his barriers.

I explain to Louis that although it's fun and all, everyone is always drunk and their biggest claim to fame is the Enola Gay.

"You mean the plane that dropped bombs on Pearl Harbor?" asks Louis, not really paying attention.

"No," I explain, "The plane that dropped the bombs on Hiroshima and stuff."

"What the fuck does Sigma Nu have to do with that?" asks Louis, now looking up from his game, as he lets his spaceship be destroyed by the little black and white guys floating above it.

I can see in his eyes he's interested.

"Well," I explain to him, "the pilot was Paul Warfield Tibbets."

"So," says Louis, "cough it up, Tabb."

I tell him that all the guys in the frat are proud of this Tibbets guy, who was a member of Sigma Nu as well. Then I tell him about this stupid book I have to memorize with stupider mottoes than the boy scouts have, and how, once a week, the brothers take turns swinging golf clubs and baseball bats at my head while in their bathrobes.

"Why do they do that?" asks Louis.

"Because I'm bad at remembering things," I answer.

Louis tells me that if they had asked him to join the frat, and he, for some reason, decided he wanted to be in it, he would be there, protecting me.

In my heart, I knew he was telling the truth.

*

Toward the end of the school quarter, Hell Week rolls around. That's the time when all the fraternities and sororities, on, and I suppose off, campus, pick who gets to stay and who gets black balled.

When I first asked Joe about that term a few weeks earlier, he tells me not to even worry about it. He explains that sometimes pledges are so bad, they are banned from the house, forever. But that wasn't going to happen to me. No way. No how.

I take his word for it and never gave it a second thought.

As we start having meetings every night at the run-down Sigma Nu house in the student ghetto, things get more and more intense.

One night I find myself tied up outside a sorority with my "brothers" pissing on my naked body which is strung up against an empty keg, and another night, being punched around by a bunch of guys who tell me that they're my friends and it hurts them more than it hurts me.

They sound like my father.

*

"You glad Hell Week's almost over?" Jim asks me one bright and early morning, as I stumble into my dorm room, still drunk and just having vomited next door into someone's laundry on the "spin" cycle.

"Yeah," I moan, as I lay on my cot.

"They're not making you do the elephant thing, are they?" he asks.

"No," I tell him, "they're not making me do the elephant thing, whatever that is."

As I try and shut my eyes to get even the tiniest bit of rest, Jim starts talking again.

"Aren't you curious what the elephant thing is?" he says.

"No," I tell him, "but I know you're going to tell me, anyway."

And he does.

Jim explains that when he first joined Kappa Alpha, everything went fine.

Until Hell Week, that is. Then, he tells me they made him march around campus naked, covered him with rubber tires and set them on fire, and made him do the elephant thing.

Shocked awake, I ask him what that is.

"You know how elephants all walk around in a circle at the circus?" he asks.

I tell him I do. That each elephant, with his trunk, holds the elephants tail in front of him or her.

"Yeah," says Jim, and what happens when they blow that whistle?"

"They reverse direction," I say, not really understanding what he's getting at.

"Now," explains Jim, "imagine those elephants are pledges."

"Uh huh," I say. "Whatever."

"Each pledge's left hand his stuck in his mouth like he's an elephant," explains Jim.

"Go on," I say, actually curious.

"And each pledge's right hand is his trunk," Jim continues, "which, instead of holding onto the tail in front of you, is stuck up the guy's ass in front of you."

I think about it and feel like I'm going to puke again.

"Get it?" asks Jim.

"I think," I say.

"Then they blow the whistle," explains Jim, and we reverse directions.

The thought of reversing thumbs makes me puke for the second time that morning.

*

Near the final week of the quarter, Amy, this time in a black, furry cowboy hat and alligator boots, stops me.

"George," she says, "I gotta tell you that even though you've still managed to show up to *every* class, you are still failing bowling."

I ask her how that can be, and she explains that even though my attendance is perfect, my bowling scores are not.

"If you don't pass the final," she tells me with all seriousness, "I'm going to have to fail you!"

I ask her what I can do to stop this from happening and she hands me the bowling textbook I never bothered to buy. It's 246 pages of statistics, etiquette, and proper bowling technique.

"Read this and take the test," Amy tells me, "if you pass with an A, I'll give you a D."

I think about it.

A lot.

And two days later, when it's time for the final, I grab that little answer sheet, and with my number two pencil, make the shape of a bowling pin out of all those tiny bubbles.

Of course, I fail.

When asked a couple of days later by Amy, who seems to really have taken a liking to me, why I'm so self-destructive and why I chose to give myself a failing grade, I break it down for her and her cowboy hats.

"It's like this," I tell her over a cup of coffee at a small table in the corner of the student union. "If I get a D, it looks like I tried. Which I did. I showed up every damn morning there was a class, and you know that."

"Uh-huh," says Amy, "go on."

"But if I get an F, that means I fail. And no one ever has to know that I tried and failed bowling."

"I like your way of thinking," says Amy, and even though she still gives me a failing grade, we become friends later in my college career.

*

A week before that fateful party with the Sigma Nus and the Tri Deltas, I find myself in Daytona Beach for the night.

Screaming "Road Trip!" Joe, Wally, and a couple of the other guys decide we should drive the hour and a half to some topless bar, where we end up drinking ourselves into a stupor.

As blondes, brunettes, and redheads parade around naked in front of me, I'm not sure whether to puke from the booze or hump one of the girl's legs like Joe says it looks like I'm going to do.

In the end, it looks like I'll get to do both as the guys invite the girls to our hotel, and they accept.

On the way, I keep telling Joe, Wally, and whoever will listen that this is the best night of my life. That tonight, *after* I throw up, I'm going to have sex.

Wally, or someone, tells me to take another shot of the Wild Turkey they've got in the glove compartment, and the next thing I know I'm waking up in an unfamiliar bathtub covered in vomit.

I try to reconstruct the previous night's events, but everything becomes dark and murky after the whiskey.

As I stare at my blue jeans, Nike All Courts, and black leather jacket, all covered in vomit, the stench starts to make it's way up my nose.

Then I begin to remember the dreams I was having sometime earlier.

About me.

On a surfboard.

Riding it on a lake of flames.

Beneath me, engulfed in fire, is my father, stepmother, all those Crossroads Church of Christ kids, and Louis. They're all screaming in pain as I notice a small figure next to them.

It's a boy.

He's got curly brown hair and is strangely silent.

And crying.

As his tears make their way down his fat little cheeks, I feel them wash over my feet, which are bare, like the rest of me. The warmth from them feels good as I continue to surf atop the flaming lake, for some reason smiling and completely naked.

The smell of upchucked seafood awakens me from the thoughts as does the sound of barfing.

I look up and see Wally, as well as one of the strippers, puking on my legs.

It feels warm.

It's then I realize that the vomit I'm covered in is not mine, and I scream.

*

So there I am, in my black leather jacket, which the guys in Sigma Nu have asked me to stop wearing from tomorrow forward.

While I don't like that idea at all, I've got bigger things on my mind to worry about.

This blonde girl has just rejected me twice, and now Wally and Bob, as well as Todd, are all giving me the evil eye.

As I walk toward them, I explain that the Tri Delt girl has once again rejected me, and this time, with a racial insult.

"Look, George," says Wally, "I'm gonna give you one more chance. You talk to her or you're out!"

That's when my friend, Chris, the United States Marine, decides it's time to step in and help me.

We both walk up to the blonde who is busy with her friends and I clear my throat.

"Ahem," I say, desperate, "I know you hate me and all, but please try and make it look like you are talking to me. Please?"

Chris explains to the girls that I'm a pledge, and it's important for me to look good in front of my brothers. He explains that he too, was once a Sigma Nu, and is now serving his country overseas.

"They should have gassed all you Jews or cooked you in the ovens," screams the girl.

Really shocked, neither Chris nor I say anything.

Finally I get up the nerve to say something, but decide to spit it, instead.

Right in her blonde haired, blue-eyed plastic surgery disaster of a face.

I hurl the largest loogie I can and it lands on her upturned little pig-nose, before dripping into her mouth.

"Why you little fucking kike," she starts, "why don't you and your dumbass Marine friend here just leave this party now. It's obvious nobody wants you here."

I look toward Joe and Wally, who give me the thumbs up signal for engaging in a conversation with this moron.

"Excuse me, ma'am," says Chris, in full uniform, "did you just say the words 'dumb Marine'?"

"You heard me, jarhead," sneers the little bitch.

"Well ma'am," Chris explains rather politely, "you have just insulted a member of the United States Armed Forces. And by doing so, you have not only done damage to myself and my friend George here, you have used slanderous words against this mighty country, America. A beautiful and free country."

As he's saying all this, I swear I can hear that Francis Scott Key song playing on the stereo instead of some awful disco.

"And that," continues Chris, "I find to be treason. So, in accordance with United States Marine code seven four nine seven, I find you guilty and shall hereby deliver your punishment."

By this time everyone is staring at us, because, I realize, Chris is screaming.

At the top of his lungs.

Wally's and Joe's faces both have very confused looks on, as does the little Tri Delt.

That is, before it's met with the crushing blow of Chris's fist, which not only instantly breaks her nose but sends her flying back five feet as well.

"Holy shit," I hear myself yell, and suddenly everything seems to go into slow motion.

Chris yells for me to follow him on foot, and I do. As fast as I can.

We run to the parking lot where he's parked his Chevette and jump into the thing. After Chris starts it, he does a 180 into the oncoming mob of angry Greeks.

They jump out of the way of Chris's car as he yells a mighty "Ho-Rah!" and we speed off into the night.

At first, we find ourselves being tailed, but Chris, the expert Marine he is, soon loses whoever has decided to follow us.

Back at my dorm a half-hour later, as Chris drops me off, I ask him one simple question.

"Why?"

"Because," Chris tells me, "I don't really like those guys, anyway. They're sorta jerks, huh?"

I nod my head as Chris tells me it's been swell knowing me, then burns some rubber as he races off into the hot Florida night.

*

As I enter my dorm room I see my roommate, Jim, hanging up the phone.

"Guess who that was?" asks Jim, with a silly smile on his face.

I tell him I don't care.

"Does the word blackball meaning anything to you?" he says.

I think about if for about an entire second, then tell him my answer.

"No," I say.

Then, after getting undressed, I get the first good night's sleep I've had in a very, very long time.

SURFING ARMAGEDDON

SO THERE I AM at the check-in desk at the Econo Lodge Motel on Southwest Thirteenth Street in Gainesville, Florida.

Standing to my right is Andrea. She likes the punk rock. I can tell from the Devo and Undertones buttons she's wearing on her black jean vest. That and I guess the dyed green bangs on her head.

The clerk behind the desk looks at us funny over his wire-rimmed reading glasses.

"What was that name again?" he asks.

"Ramone," I say. "Dee Dee Ramone".

"Is that spelled capital D, and capital D?" he asks.

"D-E-E space D-E-E," I tell him.

"Ramone?" he asks. "Is that one of them there Hispanic names? We don't want no trouble."

I tell him there won't be any.

"And her?" he asks looking directly at Andrea, who is busy trying to get free gum out of the Elk's Lodge gum ball machine.

"She's my wife" I say.

"That would be Mrs. Ramone?" he asks.

I tell him he's pinned the tail on the donkey.

"Does she have a first name?" he asks.

"Sheena," I say "S-H-double-E-N-A".

The clerk writes the names down on his registry sheet and gives us the key to the room.

"You are in room number thirty-one," he explains in his silly work jacket that says "Earl" in scripty letters next to the motel's logo.

"Uh huh," I say.

"That's downstairs and to your left when you walk out of this here office," he explains, "and I don't want no funny business in my motel, Mr. Ramone!"

Again, I assure him there won't be.

"Good," sighs Earl. "And I sure as hell hope you two is married, because if you weren't, well you'd be sinning. And God don't like sinners."

I assure him that we are in fact married and we just need a good night's sleep.

He tells us he's glad, then goes back into his back room where we hear him turn up *Hee-Haw* on his television.

I look over at Andrea, who is still busy with her finger up inside the gum ball machine.

"We've got the room," I tell her.

She smiles.

That kind of sexy smile.

Then she says, "Great, let's go, but first help me get my finger out of this fucking machine."

*

As we both approach room number thirty-one, my heart starts to beat really quickly. And my stomach starts to hurt. Plus, I'm sweating.

And the one hundred plus temperature outside doesn't help things.

"You have done this before?" Andrea asks me for like the fifth time that day.

I tell her that of course I have.

"Okay," she says. "You just look kinda nervous."

I tell her it's just the heat, what with me wearing my black leather jacket and all.

She just smiles at me.

We reach room number thirty-one of the Econo Lodge Motel, and I try putting the key in the keyhole, but it won't fit.

Andrea, smoothly, takes the key from my sweaty hands and slides it in.

Easily.

"Are you sure you have done this before?" Andrea asks for the sixth time that day.

I ask her to please quit asking me that question, and that of course I have.

"I'm twenty-two," I lie. "How many twenty-two year old virgins do you know?"

She smiles as she opens the door and we feel the cool breeze of the air conditioner sweep against our skin.

"Well," she says, "let's get to it!"

Just like that.

She walks over to the bed, sits down, and begins to remove her black leather boots. As she does, I just stand there and stare at her.

My brain is racing faster then my heart.

What was I supposed to do now?

Here I was, the end of my first quarter at college, at the Econo Lodge Motel on Southwest Thirteenth Street, about to hopefully lose my stupid virginity once and for all.

And I think I never felt such fear before in my life.

*

I guess it's fair to say I was a late bloomer.

Late, hell, more like I missed the fucking train.

Totally.

While others were on board, living it up, and drinking it down in the bar car, I was the guy who was sitting alone at the snow covered train station, wondering where the hell everyone went.

I'm not sure why, but I think it's because I never really understood sex.

Like, how it was done.

*

I remember as a kid, my stepmother Cybill, bringing home this Time Life pop-up book about reproduction.

In those colorfully printed pages were what looked like cut out figures of dogs, cats, chickens, and eventually, human beings.

The book explained in blurry detail how the "male" of a species planted a "seed" inside of the "female." That "seed" would eventually grow and grow, and finally a puppy, kitty, chicklet, or baby would be born.

The book went on to explain while the male of the species had a penis, which it could insert into a female's vagina, it mentioned something about that not happening with fish.

So it left me confused, to say the least.

Actually, as a child, I figured all kids were born with penises. I just figured that girls were reckless with them, and broke them off early on.

I suppose that explains why when my sisters and brothers played doctor, I'd never let the girls anywhere near my private parts.

If they couldn't take care of their own, hell if they were going to touch mine.

The book also explained what a vagina was, and showed a cartoon picture of one.

It looked like a sideways version of my grandmother Rosie's mouth. Missing the teeth and everything.

*

I think it was in second grade where I probably had my first real sexual thoughts.

There was this teacher named Mrs. Arcade, and she was hot.

She wore that blue mascara that all grown-up women back then wore, and had breasts with these round things on them. I remember once asking her why the little pointy things popped up sometimes and sometimes they didn't. She explained to me that my mom had had them as well and I used to feed from them.

Totally lost, I asked if I could try feeding from hers.

She gently blushed, and told me that that would not be appropriate. That she only let her boyfriend do that.

Which just confused the hell out of me even more.

*

Then there was Kathy Hunter.

Looking back on it now, I realize she was everything I wasn't.

She had blonde hair, green eyes, pasty white skin, and a vagina.

Or at least I supposed she did.

She sat next to me in the third grade, and for some reason, every time she'd smile at me, I'd feel my penis grow in my pants.

Sometimes it would grow so much it would hurt. And sometimes, if other kids noticed it, they'd point and laugh.

But Kathy never did.

In fact, she told me she loved me. In childish writing on a pink piece of construction paper.

I wrote her a note back on my purple construction paper saying the same thing, and the next thing we knew, we were writing each other love letters for an entire week.

Finally, I think it ended because I asked in one of those letters if maybe we could try and have puppies together.

I really wanted a baby dog, and it seemed to me if it was just the case of planting a seed inside of her, it was no big deal.

*

When I reached the age of thirteen or so, I really got into Kiss. The rock band.

Well, it wasn't me actually who first got into them, it was my neighbor, Andy. He got the *Kiss Alive* album, and invited me over to hear it.

While I thought the music was kind of silly and not nearly as fun as the album of children's songs I had with such classics as "Great Green Gobs of Greasy, Grimy, Gopher Guts" or "On Top of Spaghetti," the band members themselves looked cool as hell. They were these guys who looked like super heroes, or better yet, demons from my *Eerie* or *Creepy* magazines. The ones that gave me nightmares where'd I'd wake up screaming about decapitations. And it was wicked.

Anyway, one day I find myself telling Cybill about this rock band, Kiss. She tells me that Loggins and Messina are great, that Carole King is wonderful, Led Zeppelin the shit, but that Kiss are the worst rock band on the planet.

To back up what she says, she takes out a copy of the *New York Times'* Arts and Leisure section, from the previous Sunday's newspaper off of the living room table. The table is made of thick glass with all sorts of layers, and I remember those many hours I had spent as a child staring into the thing and wondering if life was actually the same way.

Layer upon layer upon layer.

Anyway, Cybill points out an article reviewing Kiss at Madison Square Garden.

The reviewer states in one sentence that Kiss "sounds like a cow having an orgasm."

Confused, I ask Cybill what that means.

"You mean cow or orgasm?" she asks, laughing.

Not wanting to look stupid, I explain that I know what a cow is, and that it goes moo and stuff, but I'm puzzled about the other word.

"Orgasm."

So I ask my stepmom for the definition.

After she and Diana, my stepsister, who is also in the room at the time, have the best laugh they think they've had, ever, they just point at me and laugh some more.

"You don't know what an orgasm is?" laughs Cybill as tears roll down her cheek. "You really are as stupid as your father. And probably just as functional in bed."

*

At the dinner table that night, over a meal of liver and sweet potatoes with melted marshmallows on top, my father informs me that that he'd like to have a talk with me.

Alone.

I figure I'm in some sort of trouble and dread going to his office after we finish, so I play with my food for as long as possible.

After about and hour of shoveling my food around the plate, my father looks at me angrily, so I quickly put my plate on my lap and feel Sassy and Thor, our Great Danes, gobble up Cybill's swill in a matter of seconds.

"Your mother tells me you don't know what an orgasm is," my father says to me calmly as he sits behind his large oak desk, cleaning one of his many pipes out with a fuzzy stick.

I tell him I don't and ask him why my stepmom and step-sister thinks that's so funny.

He laughs under his breath, and then tries to explain to me the birds and bees as best he can.

"George," my father asks me, "have you ever rubbed yourself to the point of it feeling great?"

I explain to him I have. That if I rub my hands really fast together, I get this warm feeling, before it gets hot.

"No," laughs my father, "have you ever, you know, rubbed yourself 'down there'?"

I can see him staring at my groin.

"Um," I stammer, then not wanting to lie, I tell him the truth.

"I've held it before while I sit on the couch or sleep," I say.

"And how does that feel?" he asks.

"I dunno," I answer. "I suppose it feels good. Or why else would I do it?"

"Exactly," my father says. "Now if you were to let's say, 'play' with it, how do you think that would make you feel?"

I tell him I don't know, so he tells me I should try. Whenever I feel like it.

*

A few nights later I find myself trying to "play" with myself. I take out my penis, and a G.I. Joe doll, and make believe they are mortal enemies. I hit my penis with the G.I. Joe doll, and then hit G.I. Joe with my penis.

It doesn't feel good.

At all.

In fact it hurts.

A few nights later, really thinking about what my father had said, about "rubbing" and all, I take that approach.

At first, I rub it gently, stroking it as if it were a newborn kitten or one of our dogs.

Nothing.

So I place my penis between both palms and rub everything together.

Suddenly, my penis starts to get hard and it feels all warm and everything.

I think I start to get what my father is talking about and continue this action for about three years.

But all I ever end up with are friction burns along the shaft and blisters on my palms.

*

At the age of sixteen, I find myself reading a Spider-Man novel. While I enjoyed the comic books more, my parents had insisted I grow up and now "read books."

The book I'm reading is called *Mayhem In Manhattan*, and it's about Spidey fighting Doc Ock, and falling in love with his girlfriend, Gwen Stacey.

As the book describes Gwen Stacey, with her beautiful blonde hair, wonderful eyes, and amazing body, something strange starts to happen.

My penis gets hard.

I mean, *really* hard.

I try to ignore it as I read about Gwen's firm breasts, then I start to think of this girl on our school bus, Winnie, who has an ass shaped like an apple.

Not realizing what I'm doing, I find my hand moving up and down against my penis, and it feels like I'm on the verge of touching Heaven.

As I rub it faster and faster, I suddenly realize that it wasn't supposed to be side to side, rolling it around like I had tried doing for the past three years.

It was up and down.

Wow.

*

The next thing I know my penis is spitting up a white fluid that looks like heavy cream you'd put in your coffee, but smells like bleach.

While it continues to pour out of my penis, covering my entire stomach until it looks like a man-made lake, I start to freak out.

"Holy shit," I think to myself, "I just broke my penis!"

Now in a panic, I throw down the Spider-Man novel and wipe up the sticky stuff with my *Lost in Space* bed sheets.

"I've really done it this time," I think to myself. "I went and broke a part of my body that can never be fixed."

I then think about death, and how, I, myself, had just caused my own.

I fully expected that within a few days after those precious moments, my penis would shrivel up and fall off and I'd be dead.

Or worse, I'd be a girl.

*

Of course, the first thing I want to do is run into my father's study and tell him what happened. Tell him to drive me to Greenwich Hospital, where maybe, just maybe, they could perform some lifesaving technique.

But I don't.

I'm quite sure that if Cybill hears about it, she'll just laugh and tell me it's all my fault and I deserve it.

So I do the next best thing.

I try and see if my penis can do the same thing again.

I figure if it can, maybe I'm not as dead as I thought, that perhaps, just perhaps, I was "special" in some sort of way.

The second orgasm drips from my chin. It seems to have erupted like a volcano compared to the first one. I taste the heavy liquid and suddenly realize that not only am I not going to die, but that I have superpowers.

Like Spider-Man.

He shoots webs from his wrists, and me? I shoot them from my penis.

I'm so happy, I make my penis do the same trick all night.

*

The next day at school I tell my friends Chris and Nikhil about my "special abilities." They inform me that they have that same superpower, and if I really want to work on improving it, I should look at issues of *Playboy* or the *Sports Illustrated* Swimsuit Edition while I'm practicing.

I try that later that afternoon, and to this day, continue to practice.

*

Anyway, so I meet this girl named Andrea up in Tallahassee near the last weekend of my first quarter of college.

We are both at this shitty redneck bar, where a stupid cover band is playing Tom Petty and Elvis Costello songs.

It's "Punk Rock" night, and I'm with my pal Louis. We had decided it was time for a road trip of our own, and without telling my parents, I snuck into town and stayed at Louis' parents' house.

We are both dressed as the Blues Brothers. We're wearing dark jackets, dark hats, and dark sunglasses.

Dark trick sunglasses. The kind that light up with little red lights, by being connected to this wire and a nine volt battery that sits in your pocket.

Anyway, we are dancing with each other, because we were too scared to ask any girls to dance. We're having a great time, and Louis makes me swear that if I get drunk, this time, he drives the whole way.

"Louis," I slur, "we are on a mission from God. Don't worry about it."

We both laugh at the *Blues Brothers* reference and continue to pogo to a B-52's song. The first real punk rock tune of the evening.

Eventually, this punky looking girl walks up to me and the words "would you like to dance" fall out of her mouth.

I'm stunned.

Or in shock. I can't tell which.

Anyway, as we hop up and down on the dance floor with the blinking lights underneath it, she asks me if I remember her.

I look at her, her green bangs, her Buzzcocks T-shirt, and tell her I don't.

"Last time you saw me," she yells, "I was wearing a Clash T-shirt. Does that give you a clue?"

I think about it and try like hell to remember a girl this cute in a Clash T-shirt. But the only thing that comes to mind is a nipple.

A round, red, succulent nipple.

Then it hits me.

She's the girl from the Ramones concert that first day of college.

I'm about to tell her I remember her, but seeing the smile on my face, before I can speak, she sticks her tongue down my throat.

The next thing I know we are going at it hot and heavy on the dance floor, and Louis is just watching us embrace and kiss as he smiles.

When the song is over, I introduce Louis to our little Clash T-shirt wearing friend from the Ramones concert and he asks her how it's going.

She explains to us that she attends Florida State University, here in Tallahassee, and there are no good "men" like us in town.

She further tells us that when she was in Gainesville to see the Ramones, she thought we both were really cute.

"Really?" asks Louis, from behind his blinking Blues Brothers glasses.

She asks us if she can introduce us to a friend of hers, and the next thing I know, Louis is making out with this tall blonde girl whose name I never caught, while I get busy with Andrea.

At the end of the evening, Andrea pops the question.

"What are you doing next weekend?" she asks.

"Why?" I ask her. Stupid.

"I want to know if it's okay if I drive down to Gainesville so we can spend the weekend together," she tells me.

Not able to speak, Louis answers for me.

"George would love that," he says.

She gives Louis her phone number, and Louis gives her mine.

Still too much in shock to say anything, I just watch as they arrange a time and place where we'll meet up.

*

During the whole next week, I walk around with a permanent hard-on.

I'm finally going to get laid and I somehow know it.

Probably because of the last words Andrea whispered in my ear that evening in Tallahassee.

In little more then a sexy gasp she had told me "Fuck you later."

*

As the big night approaches, I tell Jim that this beautiful girl named Andrea is coming to stay with me for the weekend, and if possible, could he please sleep somewhere else.

"Nope," says Jim.

"Why the fuck not?" I yell. "I'd do the same for you."

"I can't," says Jim, with a serious look on his face.

When I ask him why, he informs me that his parents are due to arrive the same weekend, and it wouldn't look good with me being in a bed with a girl and all, especially since I was a Jew.

Understanding Jim, and feeling bad for him, I tell him I'll make other arrangements.

The Friday afternoon that Andrea is due in town, Doc and Rich, my neighbors across the hall, wish me luck.

"Have fun, George," they tell me, "and don't forget protection. You don't want any unwanted kids."

Thanking them for their best wishes and not knowing what the hell they're talking about, I make my way back across the hall to find Jim in our room with guests.

His parents.

His father, who looks exactly like his son, only older, is standing there in dusty blue jeans and a buttoned-up flannel shirt. His mother wears her hair up like they did in the 1950s and has a long skirt on.

They look at me as I look at them.

Then Jim's father speaks.

"Are you George?" he asks.

When I tell him I am he responds by punching his son as hard as he can in the face.

Jim, crying, looks stunned.

"You live with a fucking Jew and you didn't tell me," screams Jim's father, Mr. Summers, "you fucking little no good piece of shit."

"Why didn't you tell your father?" screams Mrs. Summers.

When Jim opens his mouth to say something, his father hits him in it again.

"Son," he screams, "haven't I taught you that Jews are the offspring of Satan?"

Jim just nods his head as he holds his jaw, which is beginning to swell.

"Haven't I taught you that they drink the blood of children and belong in Hell?" Mr. Summers screams at the top of his lungs.

At that moment I look into Jim's eyes and he looks into mine.

And for the first time, I see him exactly the way I see myself.

A mixed-up kid with a more mixed-up father.

I feel horrible for him, and as I make my way out of our dorm room that day, I'll know never forget that look of grief on his face.

*

So there I am at the check-in desk at the Econo-Lodge Motel on Southwest Thirteenth Street in Gainesville, Florida.

Standing to my right is Andrea.

She's wearing some punk buttons, one of which reads "orgasm addict."

I explain to the desk clerk that I am Dee Dee Ramone, and this is my wife, Sheena. Finally, after swearing we are married, we get the key to a hotel room.

As we enter the room and feel the cool air, Andrea starts taking off her clothes. I realize that this is really it.

I'm going to become a man.

Pop my cherry.

Lose my virginity.

Whatever.

And I'm so scared it feels like the cold war is going on inside my intestines.

As Andrea takes off her remaining items of clothing, a black leather bra and leopard print underwear, she gently slips in-between the covers and tells me to do the same.

I start undressing in front of her, feeling very shy. When I get down to my underwear, I slide next to her between the sheets.

"You have done this before?" Andrea asks me once again.

I assure her I have, and then she starts to kiss and rub me on all these parts of my body I didn't even know I had.

As I climb on top of her, like I've seen people do in the movies, she tells me to do it.

"Fuck me," she says gently.

And it's then, with my penis ripping a hole through my underwear, I tell her the truth.

"I don't know what to do," I say.

She gently tells me she figures as much, and informs me that the first thing I have to do is remove my underwear.

After I do, she gently guides my penis into her vagina.

*

As we make love, Andrea moans in what I can only assume to be ecstasy, over and over again.

I slide my penis in and out of her, fast at times, then slow.

This goes on for at least an hour, and soon I begin to get the gist of things. When she begins to moan harder, I go faster.

When she gently sighs, I go slow.

And the whole time I'm doing this, there's no way in hell I'm going to climax.

*

The next day and night are spent the same way.

Having sex.

When my penis isn't inside her vagina, I find my mouth near her crotch, and her mouth near mine.

While it's very exciting, and my heart races at speeds I never knew existed, I still can't climax and begin to wonder why.

As I make my way in and out of Andrea's vagina, I begin to think of that dream I had in Daytona Beach.

The one where I was riding on a surfboard in a lake of fire.

And somehow, this felt the same.

While warm wet feelings washed over my entire body, it felt good but wrong.

Beneath me was this beautiful woman, who was not screaming while being burned by the flames of Hades, but moaning in pleasure.

And, yet, it just didn't feel right.

As I found myself surfing armageddon that day in room thirty-one of the Econo Lodge, I realized there was a lot more to life then just getting between a woman's legs, which, somehow, felt oddly familiar.

There were other things.

Love.

Passion.

Romance.

And most of all, a feeling of connection.

*

Our lovemaking ended on Sunday, after a few more hours of going at it. While I was never able to climax, I told Andrea I had every time she asked me if I did.

"You are the most amazing lover I have ever had," she tells me as her pretty green eyes look into mine.

"I think we've done it like ten hours over this weekend," she explains.

The sides of my penis feel like it, but I don't tell her as much.

As she gets dressed in front of me for the last time, she tells me she thinks she's in love with me and to look her up in Tallahassee when I get there for the summer.

I tell her I will.

*

Later that night, I find myself masturbating furiously on my dorm bed as I'm alone in the room.

By this time I'm in total pain, and if my penis doesn't explode, I will.

I think of Andrea, her vagina, her firm breasts, and round ass.

But nothing happens.

I then begin to think about Gwen Stacey from that Spider Man book all those years ago, and the next thing I know my semen is splatting against the ceiling.

Suddenly I hear a key in my door turn and then Jim walks in.

I notice the swelling on his jaw doesn't look as bad as I thought it would, as I quickly zip up my pants without him seeing.

"So how was it, Jew?" he asks, as he sits on my bed beside me.

I tell him all about it, as I wait for my sperm, which is forming into the shape of a water drop against the ceiling, to splash down upon his head.

THE KING OF WATER OAK

SITTING IN THE BACK of my father's pickup truck with my belongings, an Irish Setter and a two hundred pound pot-belly pig that smells like hell, I'm not very happy.

My dad had promised me that when he picked me up from my first quarter of college at the University of Florida, in Gainesville, the ride back to Water Oak Plantation in Tallahassee would be fun.

He'd promised that we'd talk, father to son.

That he would tell me what was going on in his life and I'd tell him about mine.

That we'd bond.

But when he arrived that sunny Wednesday afternoon, he had my stepsister, Teresa, in the cab, and when I asked where I would sit, he said, "Go sit in the back with your pile of shit and your two new roomates."

So looking at the dog and pig, I knew this wasn't going to be the summer of love.

Two and a half hours later, upon reaching Water Oak, I climbed out of that truck, and into what I can only describe as the beginning of the end.

*

Within two days of being home, Lester and Cybill already had started on me about the whole job thing. They explained that if I wanted to live under their roof, I'd have to earn my keep.

Feelings of déjà vu should have engulfed my brain, but I was too busy building up an emotional wall to even notice a fucking thing.

So I called Henry, my old boss over at Publix, and asked for my old bag boy job back.

"Sorry, George," slurred Henry. "We can't handle all the people we've got working now. We're cutting back hours. It must be the damn economy."

So I found a job at a barn. Shoveling shit.

*

The place was called Killarn Stables and was right near the rented two room house we had lived in when we first moved to Florida.

My boss, Mary, was nice enough, what with her tight blue jeans and red cowboy boots, and it was agreed that I'd clean out horse stalls from nine in the morning to five in the afternoon. For twelve dollars a day.

And I'd work seven days a week.

While it might sound crazy to want to work so many hours for so little pay, the way I saw it was it would keep me away from my psycho parents until I was too tired to keep my eyes open.

I figured that whenever I would be home, I'd just sleep.

Plus, the idea of me shoveling horse shit for the summer not only made my father not hate me, it made him smile.

In a very weird way, of course.

*

After the second day of piling horse poop onto a pitchfork while shaking away whatever clean sawdust I could, then putting it in a wheelbarrow and lugging to a huge pile of shit behind the barn, I find myself exhausted.

"You get used to it," says Clyde, the guy I'm working with that summer whose job description exactly mirrors mine.

I look at him, all six feet five of his giant of a man and wonder if he's working for the same shit pay I am.

"How much you making?" I ask him, not knowing boundaries or much caring for them.

"Less then you," says Clyde, "you Prince Of Water Oak!"

When I ask him how he knows who I am, he explains that Mary, our boss, had told him.

"Well who are you?" I then ask.

And Clyde tells me.

*

It seems Clyde has just been released from prison, where he tells me that he had served time for second degree murder.

Of two people.

"I found my wife in bed with another man, and the next thing I knew, I'd shot a hole through the both of them," Clyde explains to me that morning as we each dig into stables full of horse shit and piss, shake away the clean shavings, then dump the waste into our wheelbarrows.

"Do you feel bad about it?" I ask, wondering if I'd feel guilt for killing someone. Like my father.

"Sort of," says Clyde, as sweat beads up on his black forehead, then works its way down his unshaven face. "I mean, she did cheat on me with her boss, but I wasn't no angel."

Clyde then tells me about the years before prison, and how he had served in Vietnam, where he had killed lots of people. He told me he shot men, women, and children.

"You never knew who the enemy was," explains Clyde, as tears began welling up in his eyes. "Once I tried picking up this five year old boy who looked like his leg had just been blown off. When I got close enough to touch him, he stabbed me in the chest!"

"Holy shit," is all I can say.

"And another time, while I was sleeping in some family's bed, they set me on fire."

With that, he showed me his back, which was covered with scars that looked like they'd hurt. Forever.

That day Clyde and I talked a lot about his experiences in 'Nam and about how he just couldn't tell anymore what was right or wrong.

I would have cried in front of him, but, somehow, I thought that was the last thing he needed.

*

After my first two weeks of work with Clyde, it is explained to the both of us that our hours have changed but pay has not. We were now to work from six in the morning to six in the evening. With no change in finances.

"That's retarded," I say to Mary. "Why are you doing this?"

"It's not my idea," she tells. "It's your father's."

Asking her what the hell he has to do with all of this, she informs me that he has purchased the barn as of two days ago, and he is now my employer.

As well as hers.

As I feel rage, anger, and now, homicidal thoughts boiling in my insides, I walk away from her, fuming.

*

An hour later Clyde finds me in a horse stall sitting on a bucket.

Crying.

"Life ain't fair, is it?" says Clyde.

Wiping the tears and snot from my face, I tell him it isn't.

"Then why not even up the score?" he asks.

I tell him that it's hopeless. That my father is fucking nuts, and I suppose he just has to have control of every part of my life.

"Don't you have a mother?" he asks me. "Besides that brown haired bitch who comes around here every afternoon to rub her pussy against a leather saddle?"

I realize he's talking about Cybill in a very mean way and really start to trust the man.

"Yeah," I tell him. "I got a mother in New York, but why would she want me? Like my father always tells me, I'm good for nothing."

Then Clyde lays it all out on the table for me.

*

"Look, Prince of Water Oak," he says, "fathers and sons always got some shit going on between them. It's the way of the world."

I just nod my head.

"Like take my own father for instance," he continues. "The last time I saw him I was two years old. My moms tells me he drank himself to death, and I don't doubt her for one second."

I tell Clyde I'm sorry about his father.

"That's not my point," Clyde kind of screams. "What I'm saying is you gotta make the best of what you got. And it seems to me you gots a mom!"

I try and explain to Clyde how I want my relationship with my father to work, and how my mother abandoned me when I was five and all, and I'm not sure I can ever forgive her.

"People make mistakes," he tells me, "it's that simple. You got to forget about them and move on."

"Huh?" I ask him, confused and feeling sorry for myself.

"Look, Prince of Water Oak," explains Clyde, "let's call it like it is. Your father, the King of Water Oak, is nothing more than a power hungry piece of shit. He'll do whatever he can to control your life. If it means buying this here barn, then he'll do it. Which he's done."

I ask him how he has all this wisdom and he just says, "You learn a lot when you watch your friends die around you in some far-off fucking hellhole. And the most important thing you take with you is who your friends are. And who your friends aren't."

I think about that.

"And your father ain't your friend," says Clyde.

I finally tell him he's right. That the guy hates me and even tells me so. He's just got me attached to him because I want to be a good son.

"And you want his money," says Clyde. "Right?"

*

I think it's at that instant that about a million pieces of a very complex jigsaw puzzle start to fit together for me.

Clyde thinks I want his money, and, in truth, I never *ever* gave that a thought. Sure he was rich as hell and had tons of the stuff, but he never gave it to me, so why would I expect it in the future?

I tell Clyde as much.

"You mean you're hanging around for some other kind of reward?" he asks me.

I start to tell him how I just want my father's respect and love. And how that's what is important to me. Not all the money in the world.

Clyde looks at me.

Then really looks at me.

I think about the words that are falling out of my mouth, and for the first time, really listen to them.

And I sound like an idiot.

*

That night, after an exhausting day of not only shoveling shit but having to listen to my own as well, I approach my father. The King of Water Oak.

"Look, Dad," I say, "I'm quitting that job at the stables, and I'm going to find another job. One that pays more."

"You can't quit," he tells me with a smile on his face. "I own the place, I'm now your boss, and you'll do what I say!"

I calmly explain to him that Mary has already told me as much, but it doesn't matter. It was time for me to take my life into my own hands and make some tough decisions. And this was one of them.

Looking at me with both a sense of respect and disgust, my father says the only thing he can.

With a tight fist.

As I sit up on the living room floor, with blood pouring out of my nose, I just look at the creep.

"As long as you live under my roof," my dad yells, "you'll do what I say."

Calmly, I tell him that perhaps it's time to stop living under his roof.

"What the fuck are you saying, shitheel?" yells my father as he kicks me in the stomach.

I think about how I spent the last summer in California, then living with my mom in New York City, and the real choices I have. Ones that I could never make before because of guilt.

Guilt about abandoning my father like my mother had done to him.

Guilt of leaving my brothers, Luke and Sam, alone with this lunatic.

Guilt about everything I have ever done or will ever do.

And I realize, for the first time, it's meaningless.

As long as I allow myself to be kicked around, I deserve it.

And if I die, I'm no good to anyone.

So I tell my father I'm leaving.

Once and for all.

*

That night, as I blast my stereo, blaring the Ramones *Road To Ruin*, I begin to pack my belongings.

As "Go Mental" plays so loudly it shakes my window panes, I get the idea I should just finish the job so I smash them out with my fists.

My blood is dripping everywhere. My father bursts into my room and demands to know what I'm doing.

I tell him I'm packing.

He yells he can't hear me, so he picks up my stereo and smashes it against a wall.

It falls to the ground in pieces.

"Where the fuck do you think you're going?" yells my father, as now suddenly everything is silent.

I tell him I'm going to go live with my mom.

In New York City.

Like I should have a long time ago.

"So that's it?" my father screams. "You're going to give up everything to go live with your mother, the junkie whore?"

With my hands still dripping with blood from the broken glass, I slug my father as hard as I can in his big fat face.

Standing there, stunned, with my red blood on his purple face, he mutters something about being right back, then leaves the room.

I write FUCK YOU in huge red letters on a bedroom wall with my dripping hands, then continue to pack.

As I'm throwing some punk T-shirts and some old Super Eight films I made into a suitcase, my father reenters.

This time with an ax.

Before he knows what hits him, I whack him over the head with a brass football statue he'd given me from many years ago.

One that he received while playing for Hofstra, some college I've never heard of.

I grab the ax that's in his right hand and put the blade to his neck.

"Got something to say to me?" I ask him, as I push the cold steel against his soft flesh.

While he remains silent, his eyes tell me everything.

In them I see fear.

And I see the tiniest of human beings.

Here was this guy, this rich guy, the king of his own castle, and beneath his rugged exterior, under layers upon layers of hate, guilt, and pure madness, was this scared little man.

Or worse yet, boy.

And that little boy was furious with me simply because I wouldn't play with him.

Play his game.
His way.

*

After I threw the ax on the floor my father stood up and warned me that if I even slept one wink that night, he'd chop me up in my sleep.

So I didn't.

I spent the rest of the night fitting whatever I thought was important to me into three small suitcases, and packed them into the back of the orange Datsun 510 station wagon with the blue Batman bat on the hood.

After one more quick call to my mother in New York, confirming my flight schedule, I made my way out to my car for the last time.

*

As I start the vehicle, I see my father about fifty yards away, in his white plantation suit.

Around him are all his workers, who happen to be black. He has them laying cement down along the sides of his driveway as he snaps his black bullwhip furiously.

I pull up next to him, then roll down the window.

"So you're really leaving?" my father asks, in the big white hat and everything.

I look at him, then at his slaves.

"Yeah," I say.

"So that's that?" he asks.

"I suppose," I say, very calmly.

"You know you can never come back, right?" says my father, rather quietly.

I tell him I do.

"Well," says my father, "it's been nice knowing you. So long."

With that I roll up my window and drive off of Water Oak Plantation for the last time.

As I look at him glaring at me in my right side mirror, I read the words printed on it: Objects in the mirror are closer than they appear.

*

It takes me many years to understand that truer words have never been written.

I tell him I do.

"Well," says my father, "it's been nice knowing you. So long."

With that I roll up my window and drive off of Water Oak Plantation for the last time.

As I look at him glaring at me in my right side mirror, I read the words printed on it: Objects in the mirror are closer than they appear.

*

It takes me many years to understand that truer words have never been written.

The author, now and in eleventh grade

George Tabb grew up one of the few Jews in Greenwich, Connecticut After moving to Florida, he started one of the state's first hardcore bands, Roach Motel, who went on to tour with Black Flag and the Dead Kennedys. Tabb later moved to New York where he played with bands like False Prophets, The Gynecologists, Iron Prostate, and Furious George. He has written or currently writes monthly column for *Maximum Rock 'n' Roll*, the *New York Press*, and the *Phoenix New Times*. He also served in the Ramones for a short time. Tabb still plays, writes, and tours, not necessarily in that order. George Tabb lives with his dog, Scooter, where ever he can in North America.

George sends thanks to: all my friends and family, the kind souls at Soft Skull, Dylan Debusk, and Sarah Loukota for the wonderful cover.